play guitar with...

the doors

Distributed By

Hal•Leonard®
Corporation
7777 W. Bluemound Rd. P.O. Box 13819
Milwaukee, Wisconsin 53213

Music compiled and arranged by Arthur Dick
Music processed by Andrew Shiels
Cover photograph courtesy of Redferns
Printed in the United Kingdom by
Caligraving Limited, Thetford, Norfolk

CD recorded, mixed and mastered by Jonas Persson
All guitars by Arthur Dick
Bass by Paul Townsend
Drums by Ian Thomas
Piano & keyboards by Allan Rogers
Harmonica by Stuart Constable

Visit Hal Leonard Online at
www.halleonard.com

guitar tablature explained

Guitar music can be notated three different ways: on a musical stave, in tablature, and in rhythm slashes

RHYTHM SLASHES are written above the stave. Strum chords in the rhythm indicated. Round noteheads indicate single notes.

THE MUSICAL STAVE shows pitches and rhythms and is divided by lines into bars. Pitches are named after the first seven letters of the alphabet.

TABLATURE graphically represents the guitar fingerboard. Each horizontal line represents a string, and each number represents a fret.

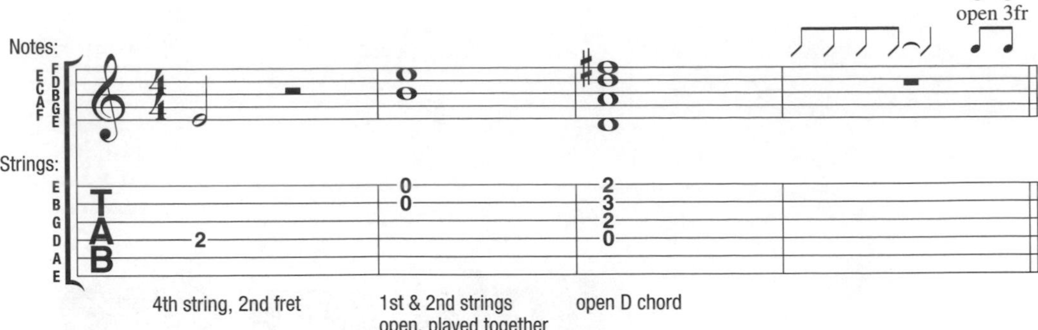

definitions for special guitar notation

SEMI-TONE BEND: Strike the note and bend up a semi-tone (1/2 step).

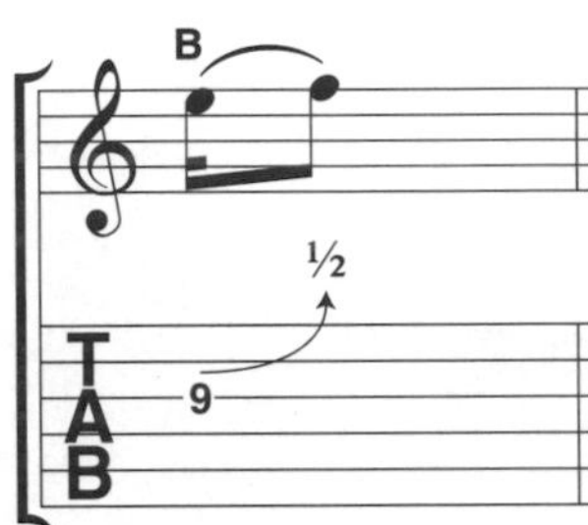

WHOLE-TONE BEND: Strike the note and bend up a whole-tone (whole step).

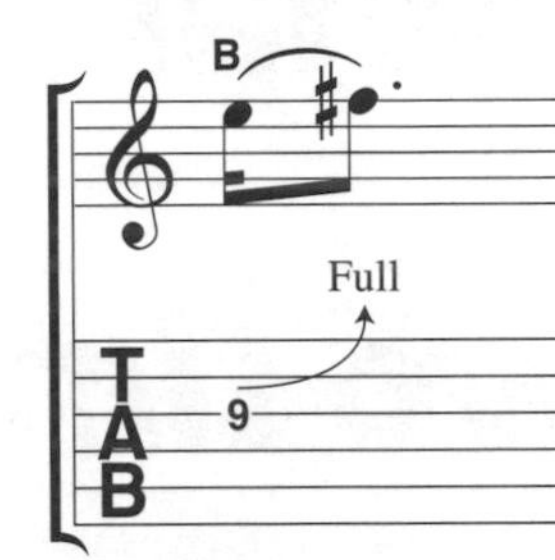

GRACE NOTE BEND: Strike the note and bend as indicated. Play the first note as quickly as possible.

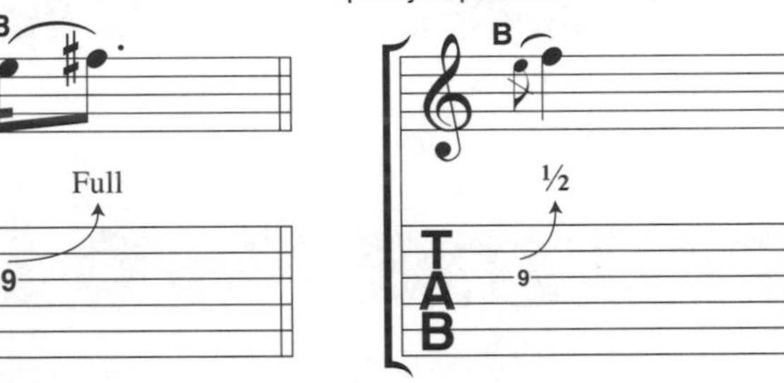

QUARTER-TONE BEND: Strike the note and bend up a 1/4 step.

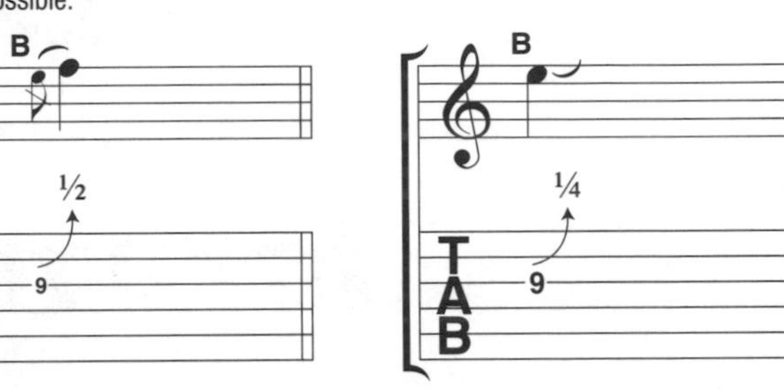

BEND & RELEASE: Strike the note and bend up as indicated, then release back to the original note.

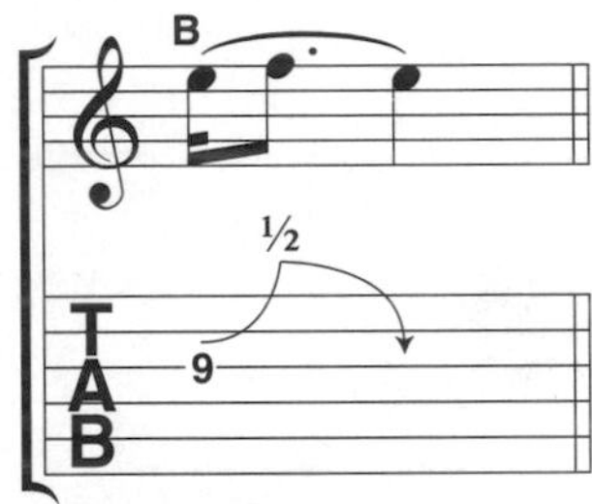

COMPOUND BEND & RELEASE: Strike the note and bend up and down in the rhythm indicated.

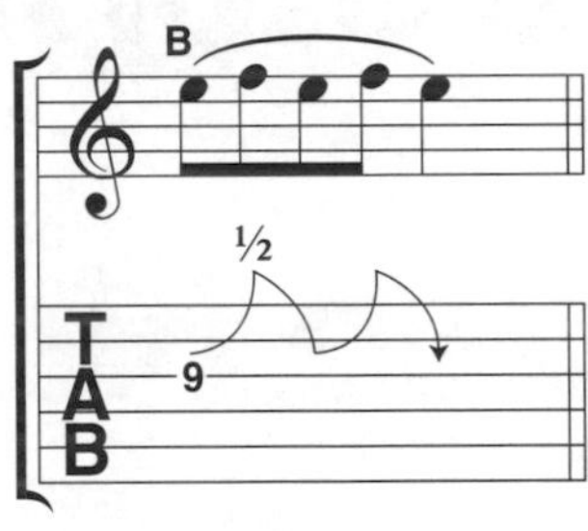

PRE-BEND: Bend the note as indicated, then strike it.

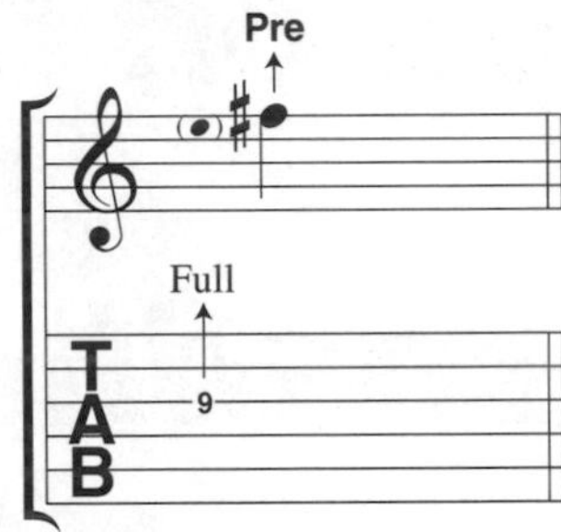

PRE-BEND & RELEASE: Bend the note as indicated. Strike it and release the note back to the original pitch.

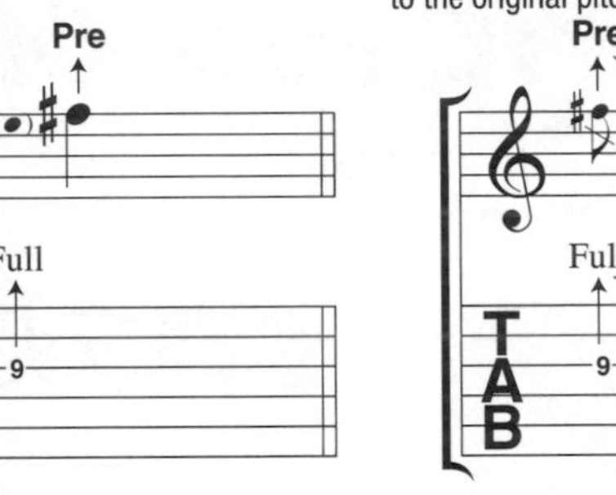

UNISON BEND: Strike the two notes simultaneously and bend the lower note up to the pitch of the higher.

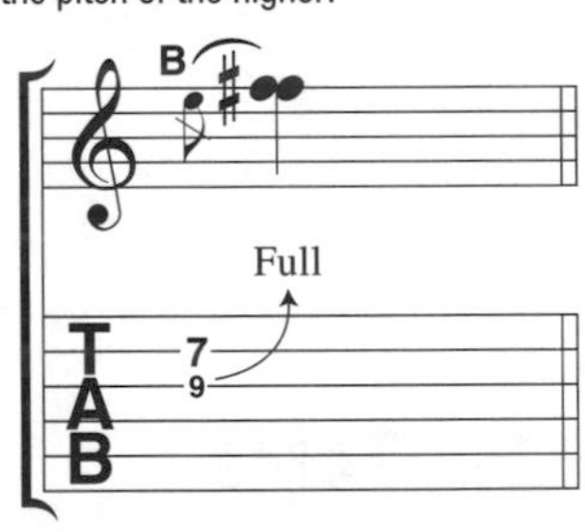

BEND & RESTRIKE: Strike the note and bend as indicated then restrike the string where the symbol occurs.

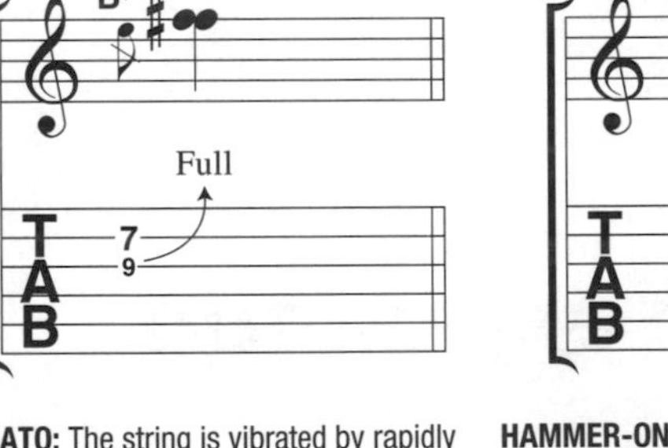

BEND, HOLD AND RELEASE: Same as bend and release but hold the bend for the duration of the tie.

BEND AND TAP: Bend the note as indicated and tap the higher fret while still holding the bend.

VIBRATO: The string is vibrated by rapidly bending and releasing the note with the fretting hand.

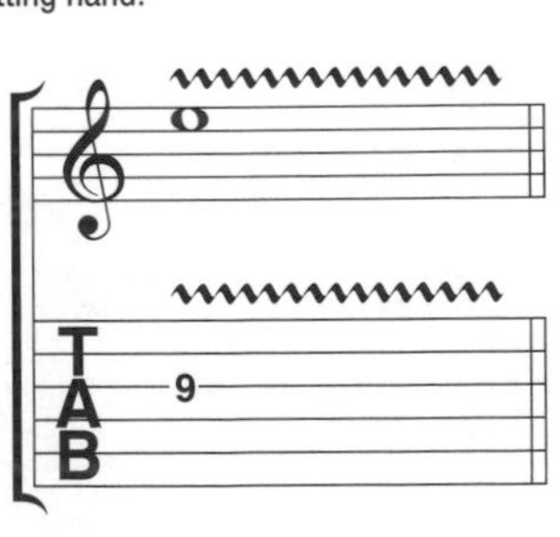

HAMMER-ON: Strike the first (lower) note with one finger, then sound the higher note (on the same string) with another finger by fretting it without picking.

PULL-OFF: Place both fingers on the notes to be sounded, Strike the first note and without picking, pull the finger off to sound the second (lower) note.

LEGATO SLIDE (GLISS): Strike the first note and then slide the same fret-hand finger up or down to the second note. The second note is not struck.

NOTE: The speed of any bend is indicated by the music notation and tempo.

SHIFT SLIDE (GLISS & RESTRIKE): Same as legato slide, except the second note is struck.

TRILL: Very rapidly alternate between the notes indicated by continuously hammering on and pulling off.

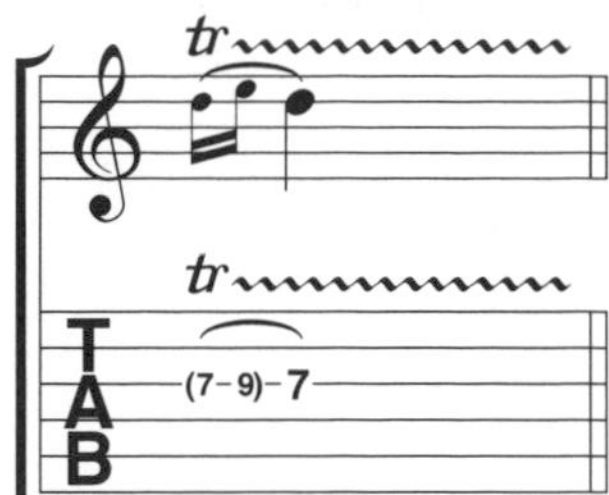

TAPPING: Hammer ("tap") the fret indicated with the pick-hand index or middle finger and pull off to the note fretted by the fret hand.

PICK SCRAPE: The edge of the pick is rubbed down (or up) the string, producing a scratchy sound.

MUFFLED STRINGS: A percussive sound is produced by laying the fret hand across the string(s) without depressing, and striking them with the pick hand.

NATURAL HARMONIC: Strike the note while the fret-hand lightly touches the string directly over the fret indicated.

Harm.

12

PINCH HARMONIC: The note is fretted normally and a harmonic is produced by adding the edge of the thumb or the tip of the index finger of the pick hand to the normal pick attack.

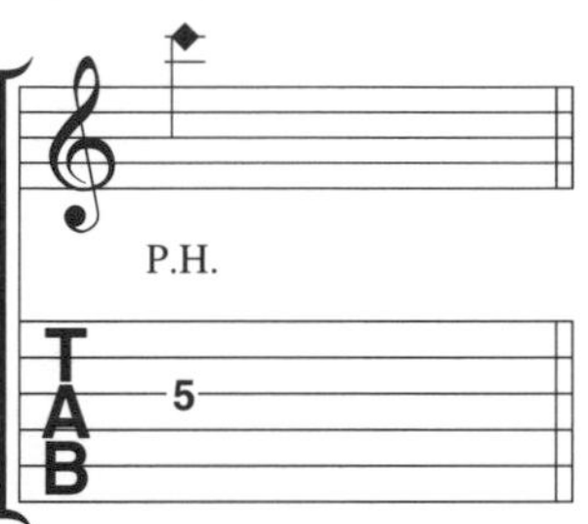

HARP HARMONIC: The note is fretted normally and a harmonic is produced by gently resting the pick hand's index finger directly above the indicated fret (in parentheses) while the pick hand's thumb or pick assists by plucking the appropriate string.

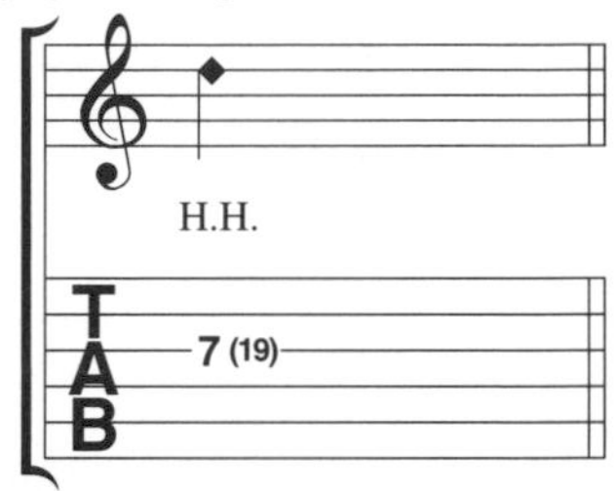

PALM MUTING: The note is partially muted by the pick hand lightly touching the string(s) just before the bridge.

P.M.

0 0 0 0

RAKE: Drag the pick across the strings indicated with a single motion.

rake

5

TREMOLO PICKING: The note is picked as rapidly and continuously as possible.

ARPEGGIATE: Play the notes of the chord indicated by quickly rolling them from bottom to top.

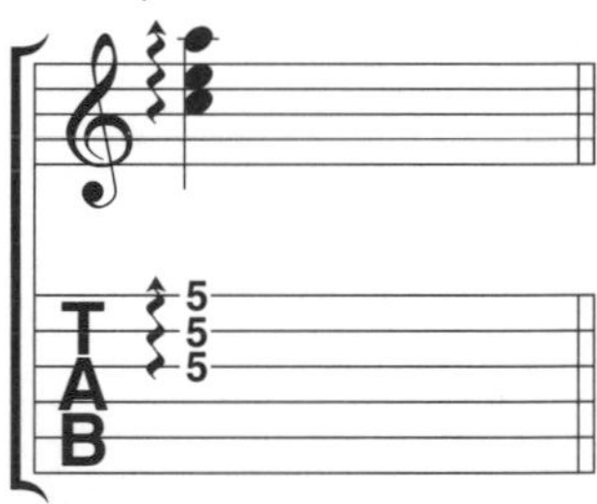

SWEEP PICKING: Rhythmic downstroke and/or upstroke motion across the strings.

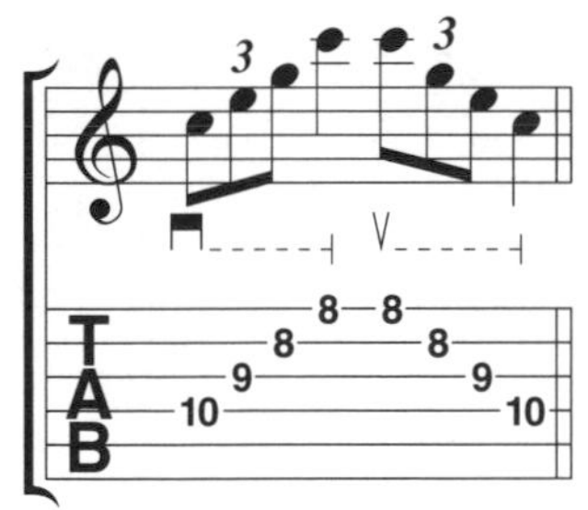

VIBRATO DIVE BAR AND RETURN: The pitch of the note or chord is dropped a specific number of steps (in rhythm) then returned to the original pitch.

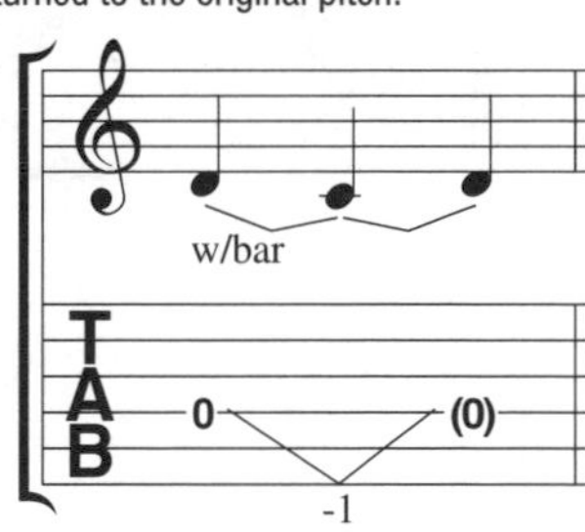

VIBRATO BAR SCOOP: Depress the bar just before striking the note, then quickly release the bar.

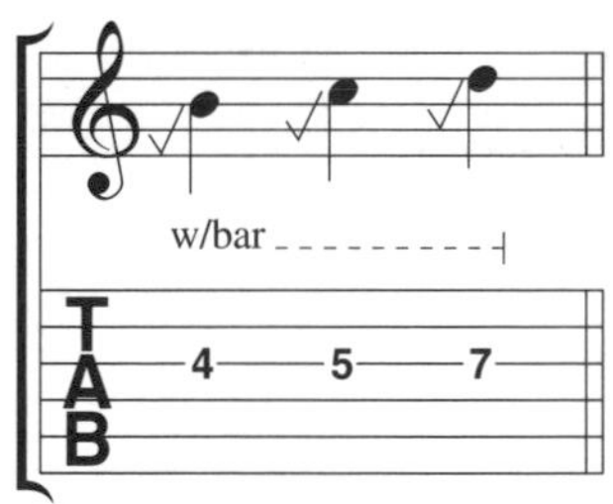

VIBRATO BAR DIP: Strike the note and then immediately drop a specific number of steps, then release back to the original pitch.

-½ -½ -½

w/bar

7 7 7

additional musical definitions

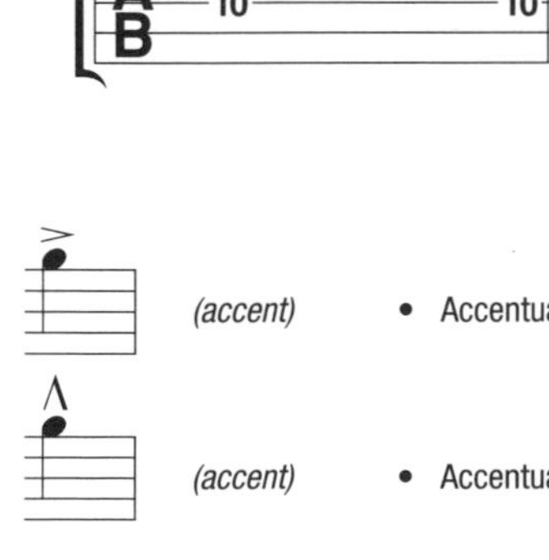

(accent) • Accentuate note (play it louder).

(accent) • Accentuate note with great intensity.

(staccato) • Shorten time value of note.

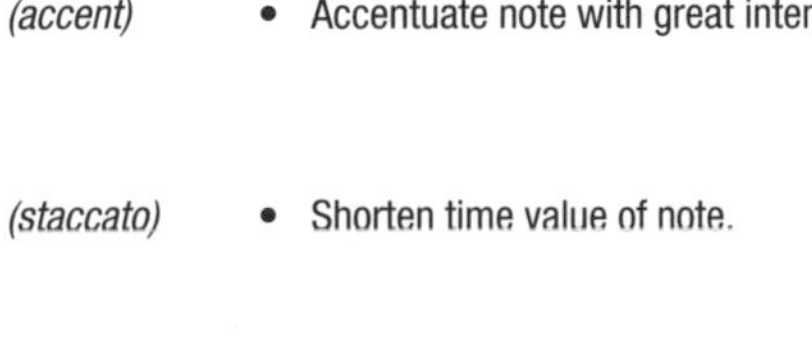

• Downstroke

• Upstroke

D.𝄋. al Coda • Go back to the sign (𝄋), then play until the bar marked ***To Coda*** ⊕ then skip to the section marked ⊕ ***Coda***.

D.C. al Fine • Go back to the beginning of the song and play until the bar marked ***Fine*** (end).

tacet • Instrument is silent (drops out).

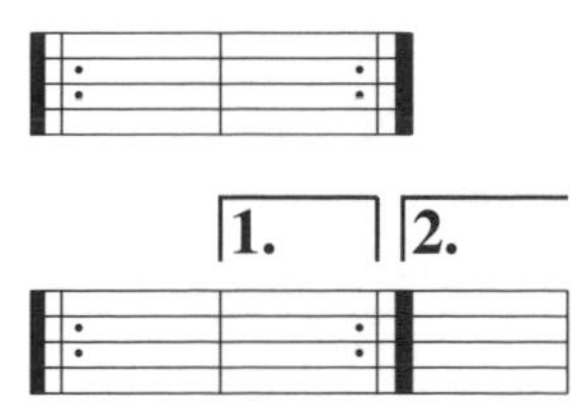

• Repeat bars between signs.

• When a repeated section has different endings, play the first ending only the first time and the second ending only the second time.

NOTE: Tablature numbers in parentheses mean:
1. The note is sustained, but a new articulation (such as hammer on or slide) begins.
2. A note may be fretted but not necessarily played.

l.a. woman

Words & Music by The Doors

Intro

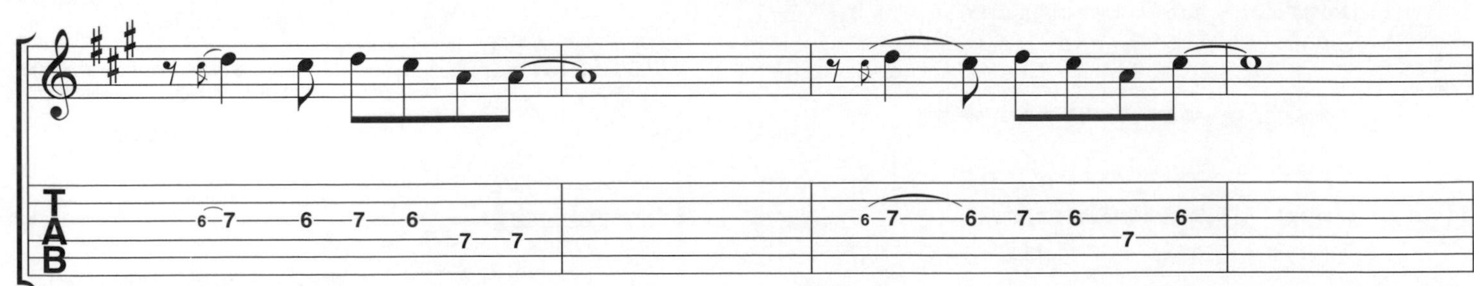

1. Well I
Verse
just got in - to town a - bout an hour a - go.
I took a look a - round see which way the wind blows.
With a lit - tle girl in a
B
¼

Hol - ly - wood bun - ga - low.
Are you a
luck - y lit - tle la - dy in the ci - ty of light?
or just an - oth - er lost an - gel?
City - y of night,
G
cit - y of night.
A
City - y of night,
G
B
¼
T
A
B

A
cit - y of night. Whoa! Come on!
Solo
A
B
Full
B
Full
Full
Full
B
Full
B
Full

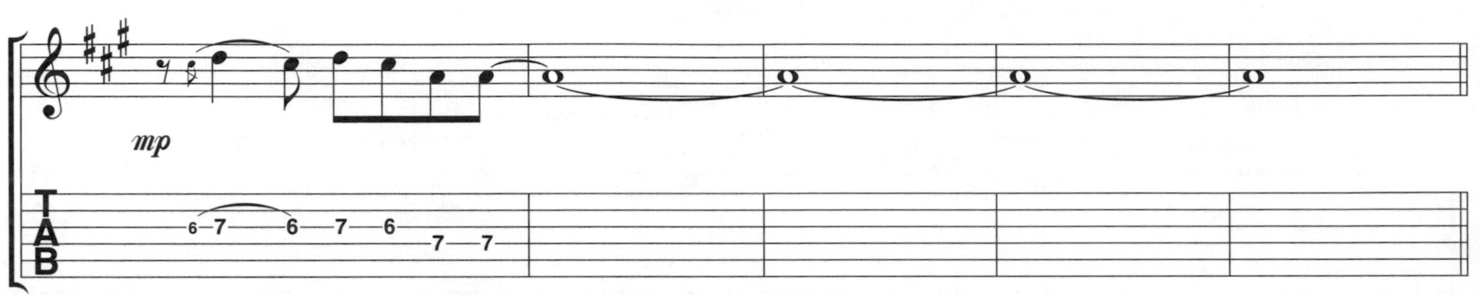
mp

Verse

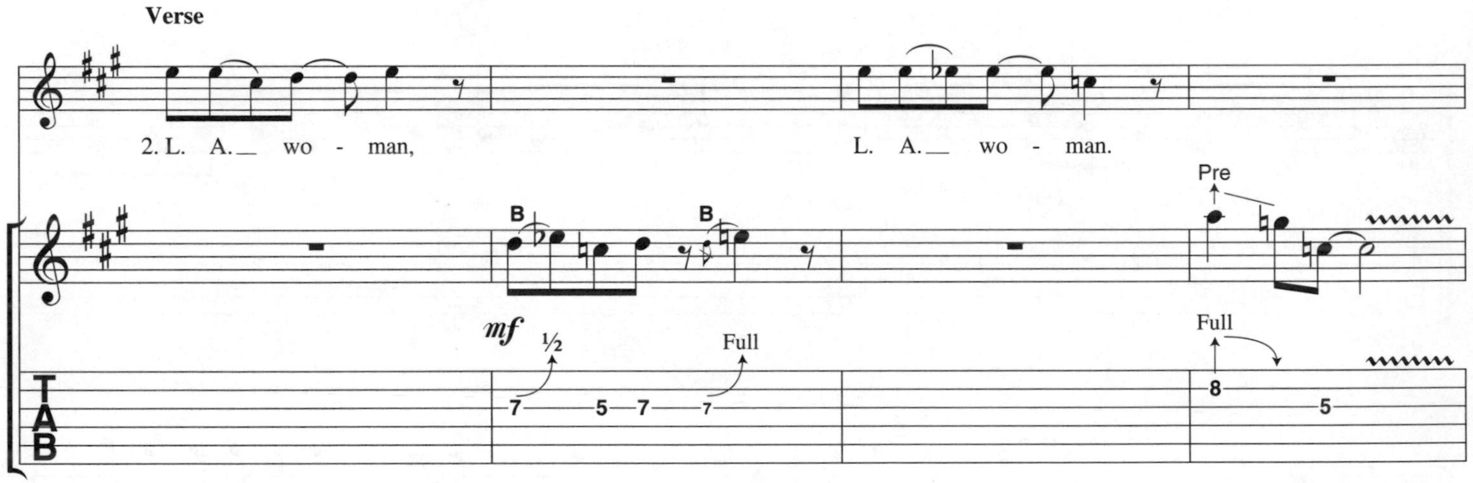
2. L. A. wo - man,
L. A. wo - man.
B
B
Pre
mf
½
Full
Full

L. A. wo - man Sun-day af - ter - noon.

L. A. wo - man Sun-day af - ter - noon.
Pre
½
L. A. wo - man Sun-day af - ter - noon,
drive through your sub-urbs
in - to your blues.
G
In - to your
A
blues yeah!
In - to your
G
blue, blue, blue
in - to your

Piano solo
Play 8x
ad lib
A
blues.
Oh
yeah!
mf
A G
1°, 2° tacet
see your hair is burn - ing,
Hills are filled with fire.
Fig. 1
1.2.3.
4.
3. I
If they
say I nev - er
know they are a
1° only
2° w/Fig. 1
loved you,
li - ar.
you

A G A G A G
Driv - in' down your free - way,
mid - night al - leys roam.
A G A
Cops in cars, the top - less bars,
nev - er saw a wo - man, so a -
G A
- lone, so a - lone, so a -
etc.

G
A
- lone,
so
a - lone.
Mo - tel
mon - ey,
mur - der
mad - ness,
a - change the mood
from glad
to sad - ness.
Full
Half tempo
Am
½

Pre
B
Full
Full

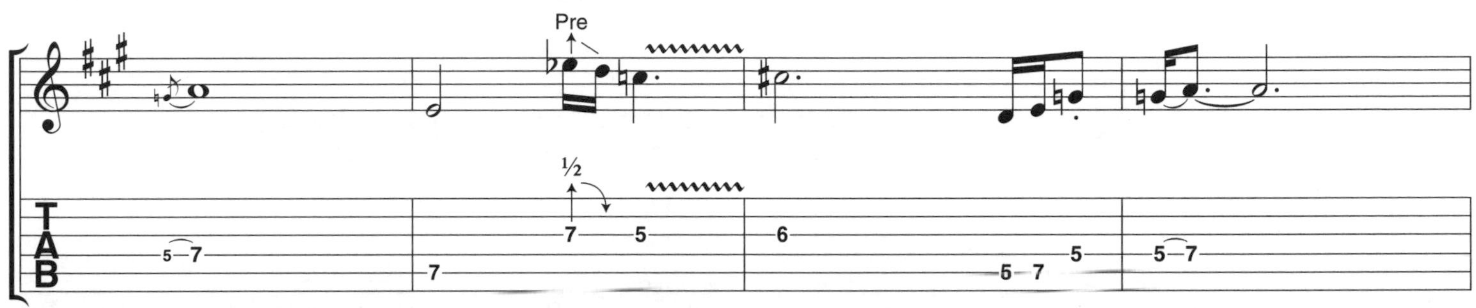

Pre
½

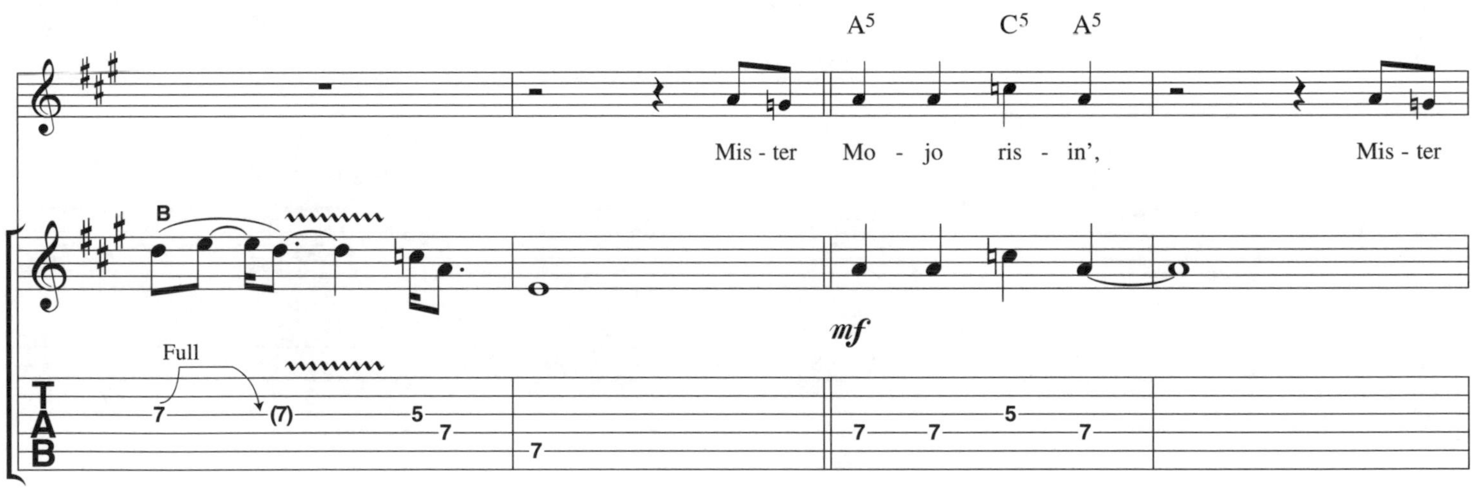

A5 C5 A5
Mis - ter Mo - jo ris - in', Mis - ter
B
mf
Full

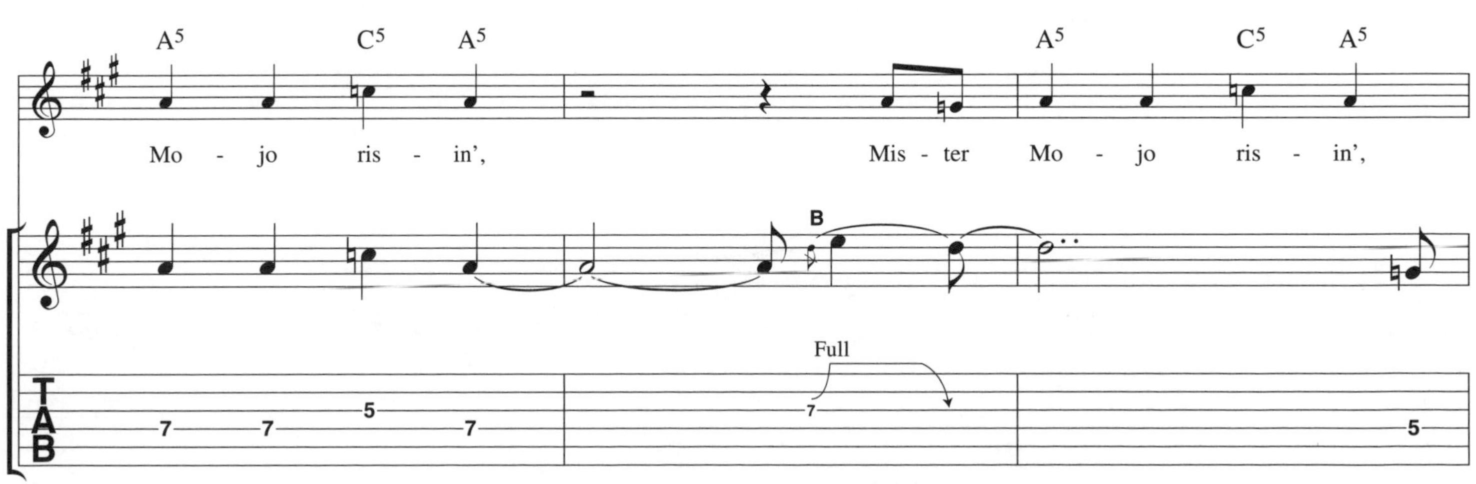

A5 C5 A5 A5 C5 A5
Mo - jo ris - in', Mis - ter Mo - jo ris - in',
B
Full

A5
C5
A5
Mis - ter
Mo - jo
ris - in'.
Got - ta
very gradually accel.
Full
keep on
ris - in'
Mis - ter
Mo - jo
ris - in'.
Pre
(A)
continue vocals sim. ad lib
Pre
Full

accel.

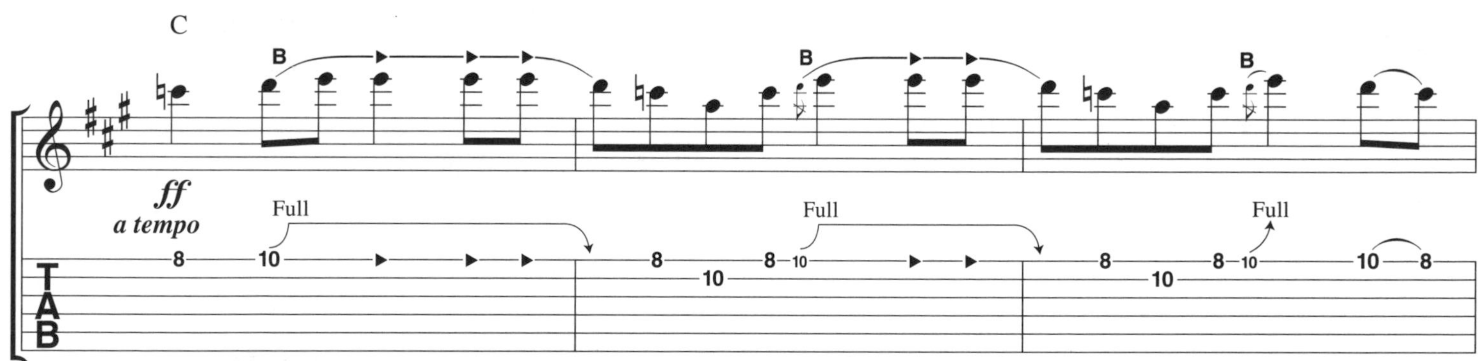
C
B
ff
a tempo
Full

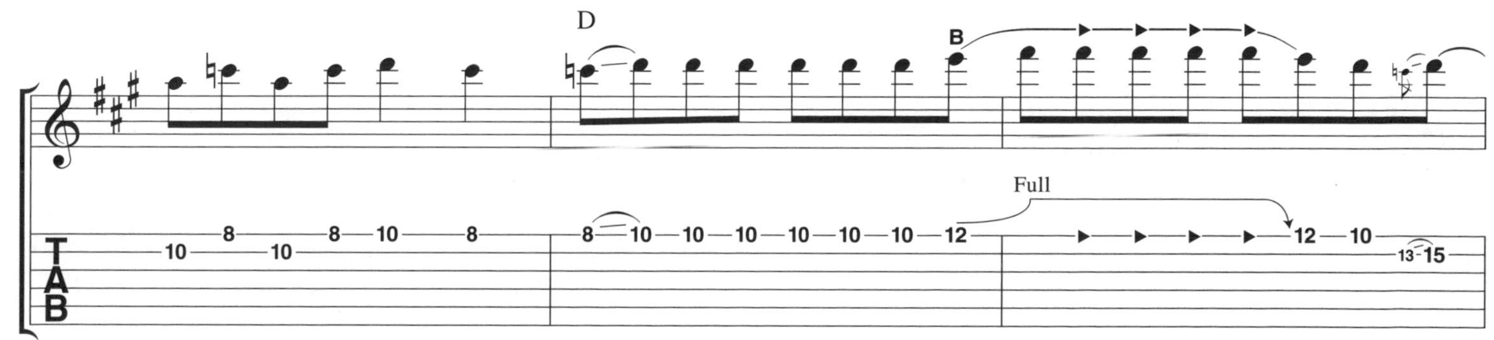
D
B
Full

A
B
Full

3.Well,

Verse
just got in - to town a - bout an hour a - go.

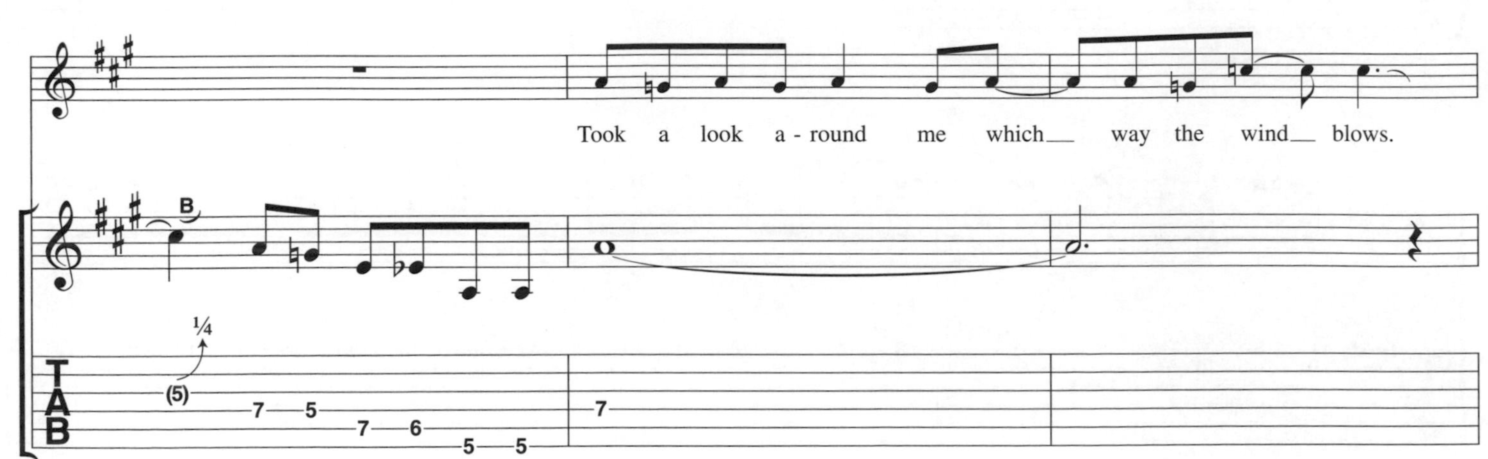
Took a look a - round me which way the wind blows.
B
¼

With a lit - tle girl in a
Hol - ly - wood bun - ga - low.
Are you a
luck - y lit - tle la - dy in the cit - y of light?
Or just an -
oth - er lost an - gel?
Cit - y of night.
G
let ring
B
¼
TAB

A
G
City of night.
City of night.
let ring
let ring
216
A
City of night!
Whoa!
Outro
A
L. A. wo - man.
L. A. wo - man.
1° vocal tacet
B
Full
B
Full
Repeat to fade
L. A. wo - man.
You're my wo - man.
w/vocal ad lib to fade
B
w/ad lib solo to fade
Full
½

light my fire

Words & Music by The Doors

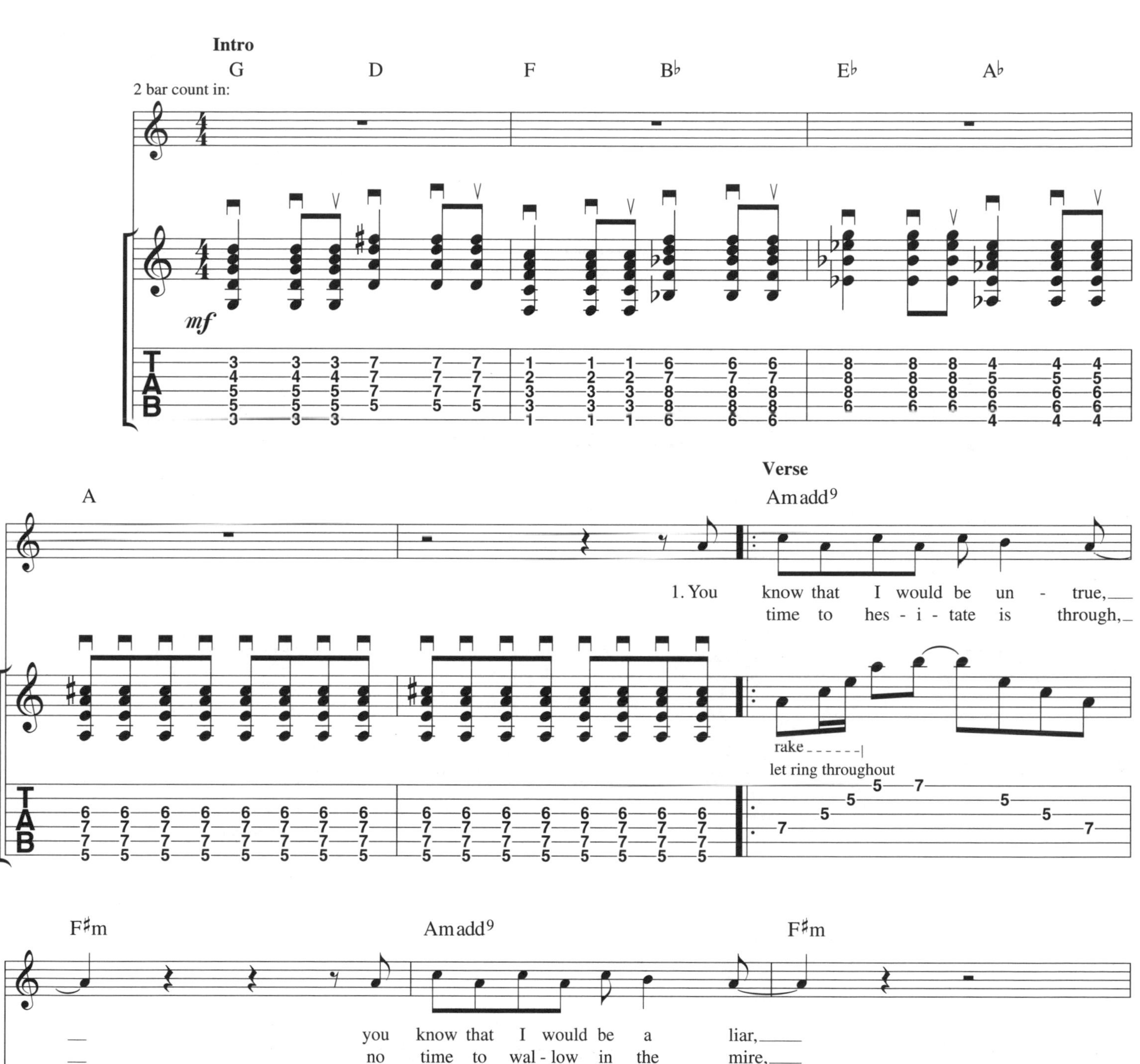

Amadd9
F♯m
Amadd9
if I was to say to you,
try now we can only lose,
girl, we could-n't get much high-
and our love be-come a fun-'ral pyre.
F♯m
Chorus
G
D
Dsus4
D
-er.
Come on ba-by, light my fire.
G
A
D
B
G
D
Come on ba-by light my fire.
Try to set the night on
1.
E
E7
2.
E
fire.
2.The
fire.
Yeah!

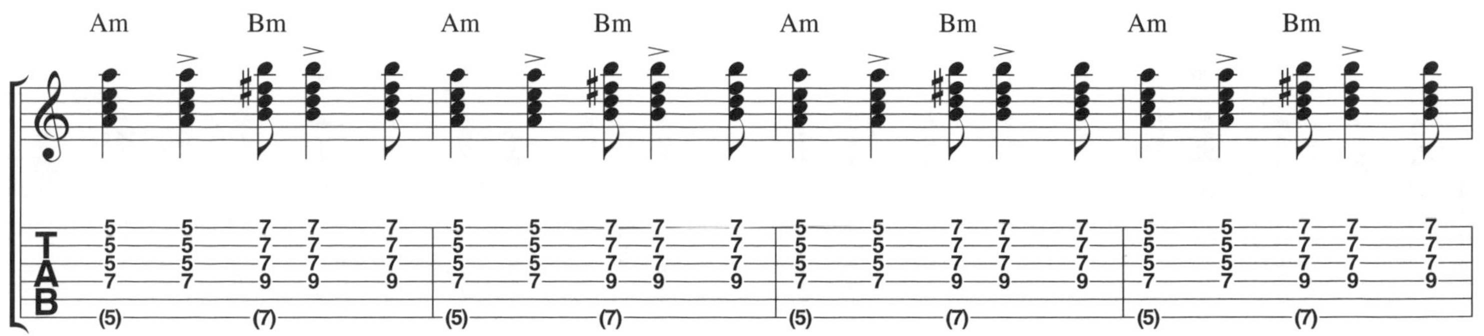
Am Bm Am Bm Am Bm Am Bm
TAB

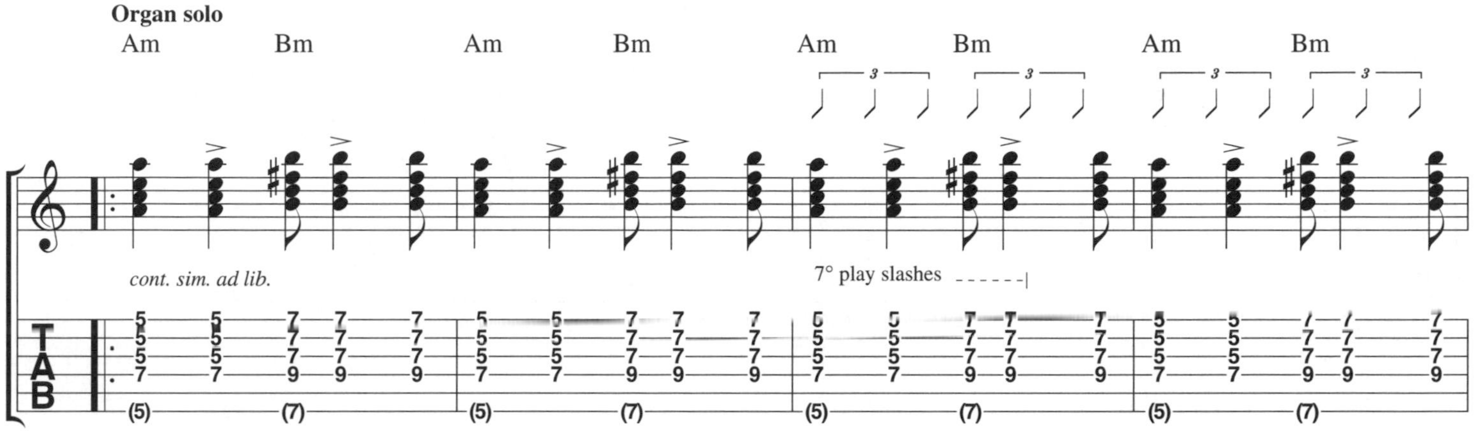
Organ solo
Am Bm Am Bm Am Bm Am Bm
cont. sim. ad lib.
7° play slashes
TAB

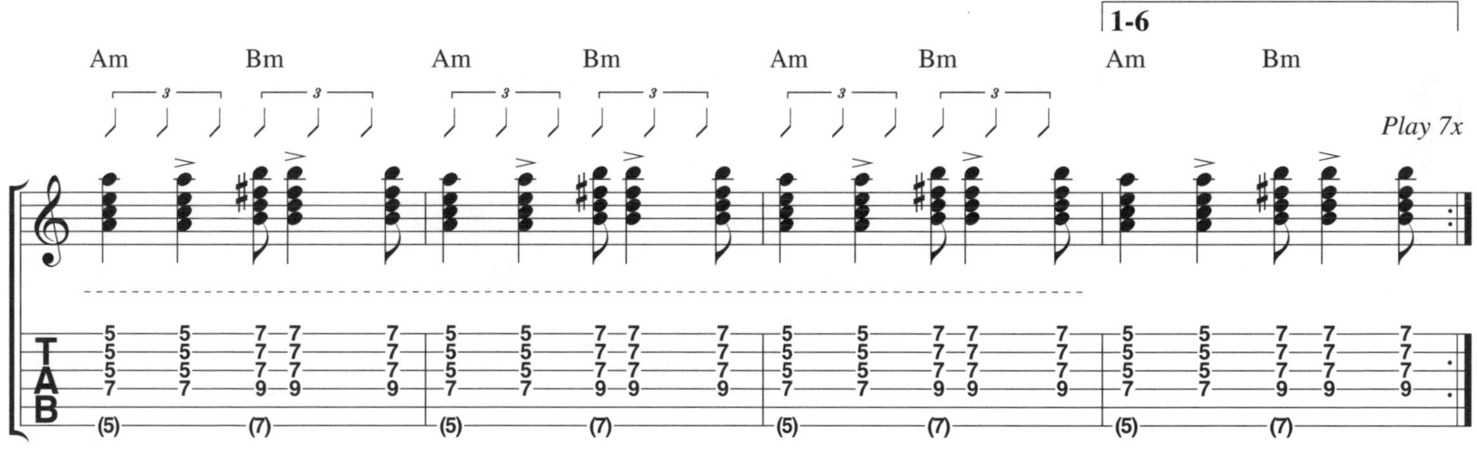
1-6
Am Bm Am Bm Am Bm Am Bm
Play 7x
TAB

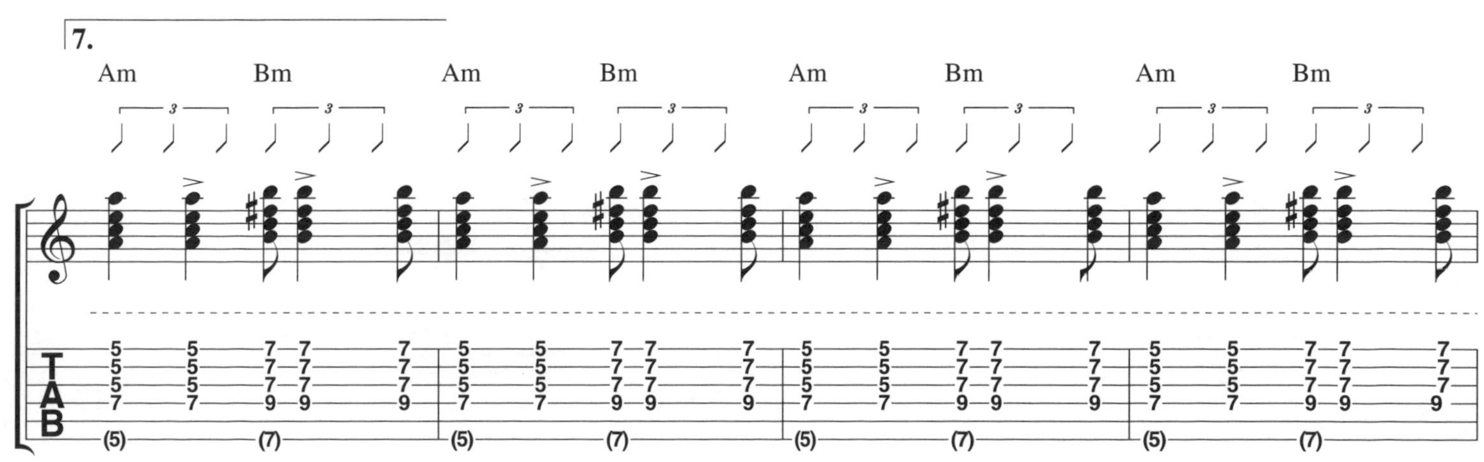
7.
Am Bm Am Bm Am Bm Am Bm
TAB

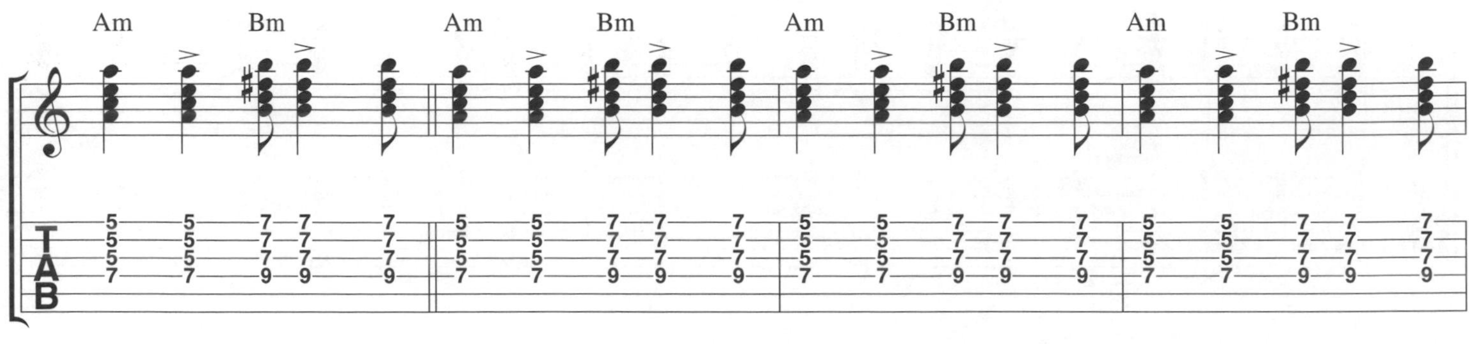
Am Bm Am Bm Am Bm Am Bm

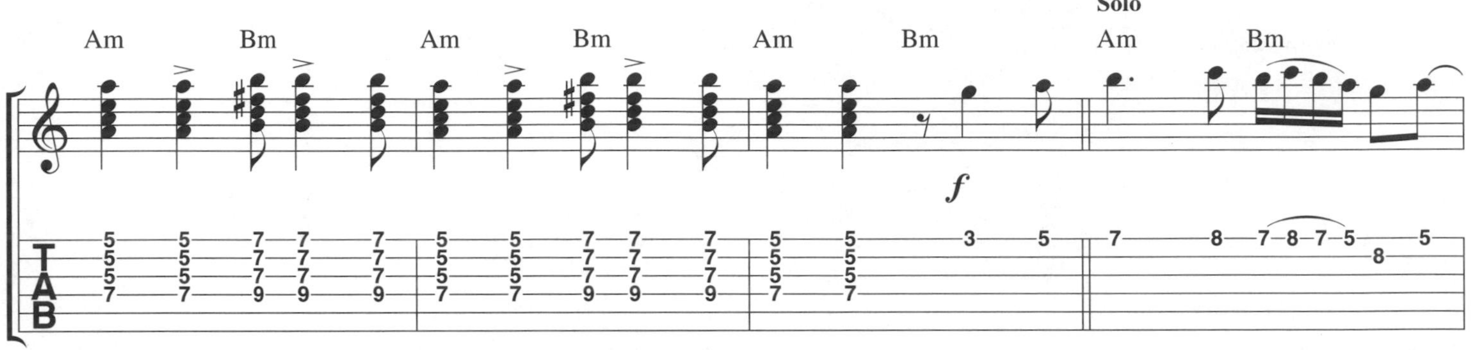
Am Bm Am Bm Am Bm
Solo
Am Bm

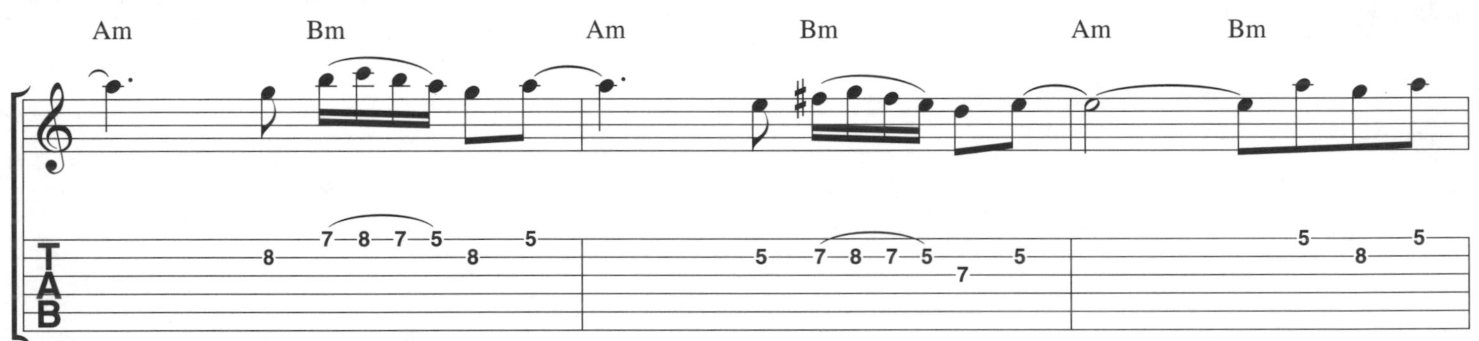
Am Bm Am Bm Am Bm

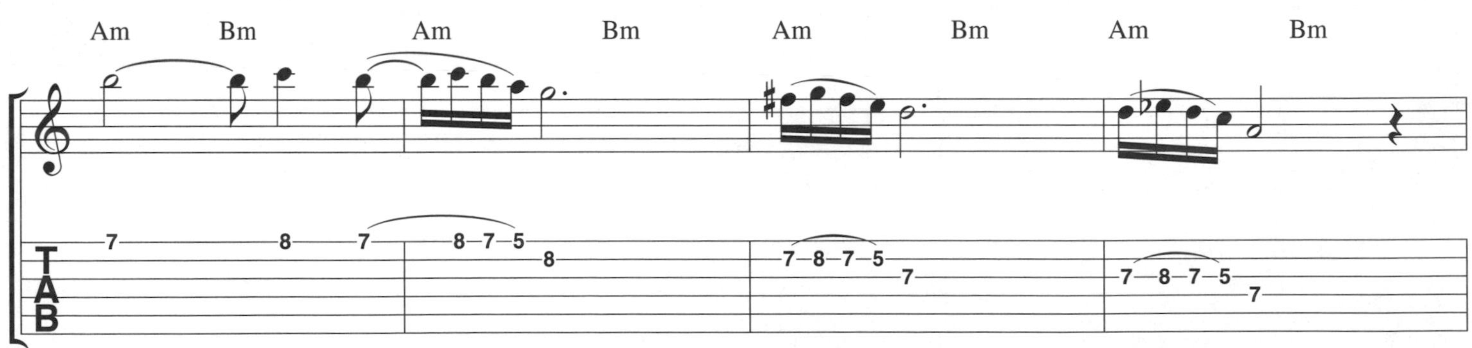
Am Bm Am Bm Am Bm Am Bm

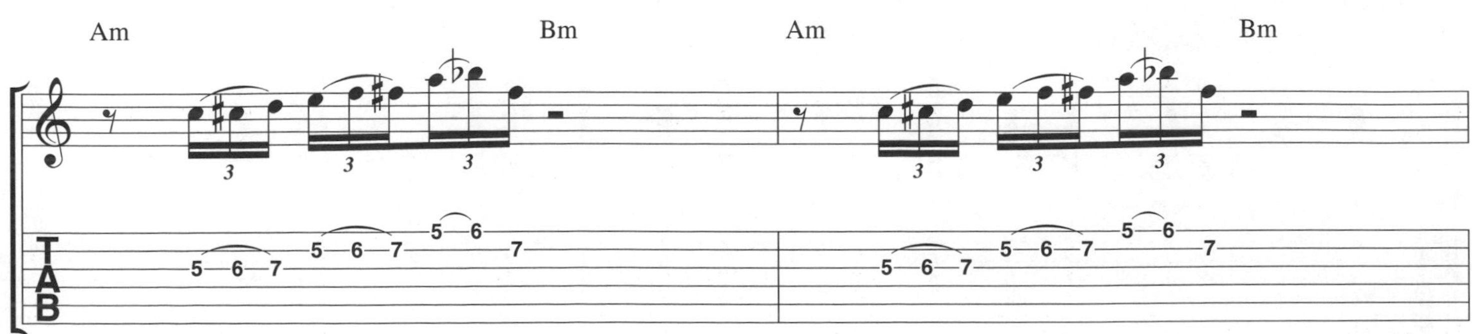
Am Bm Am Bm

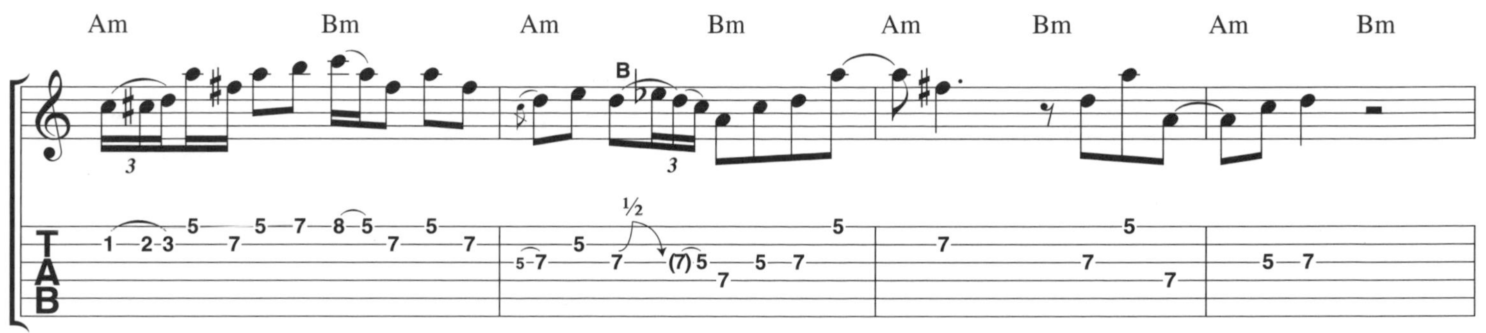
Am Bm Am Bm Am Bm Am Bm
B
½

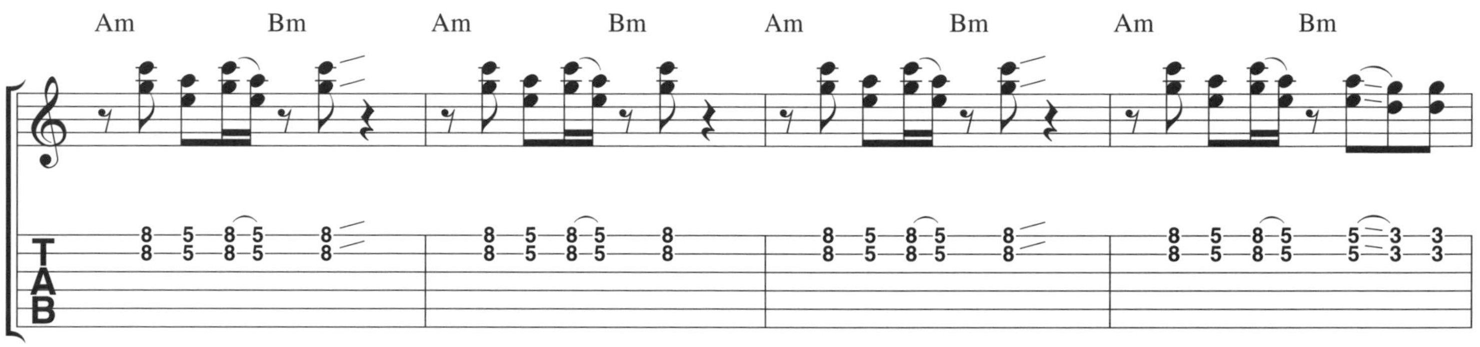
Am Bm Am Bm Am Bm Am Bm

Am Bm Am Bm Am Bm
let ring

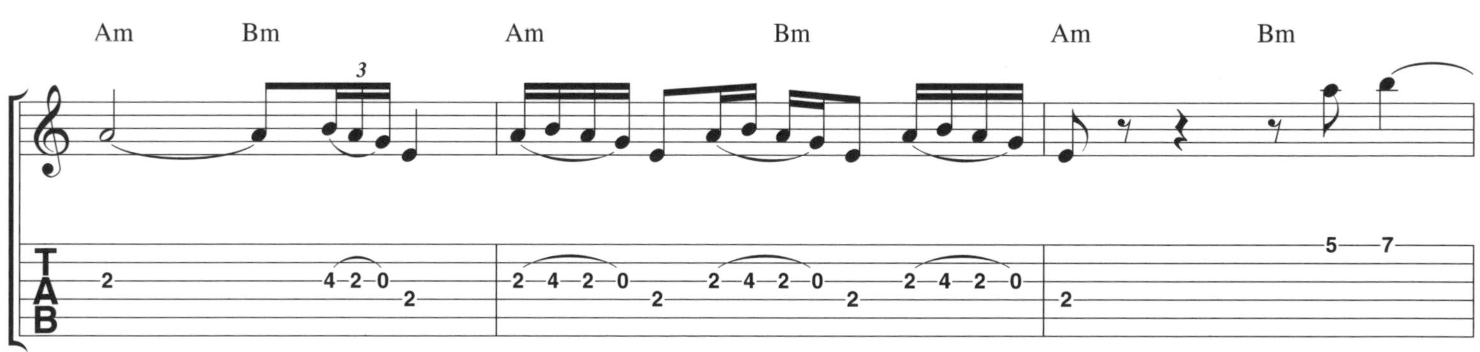
Am Bm Am Bm Am Bm

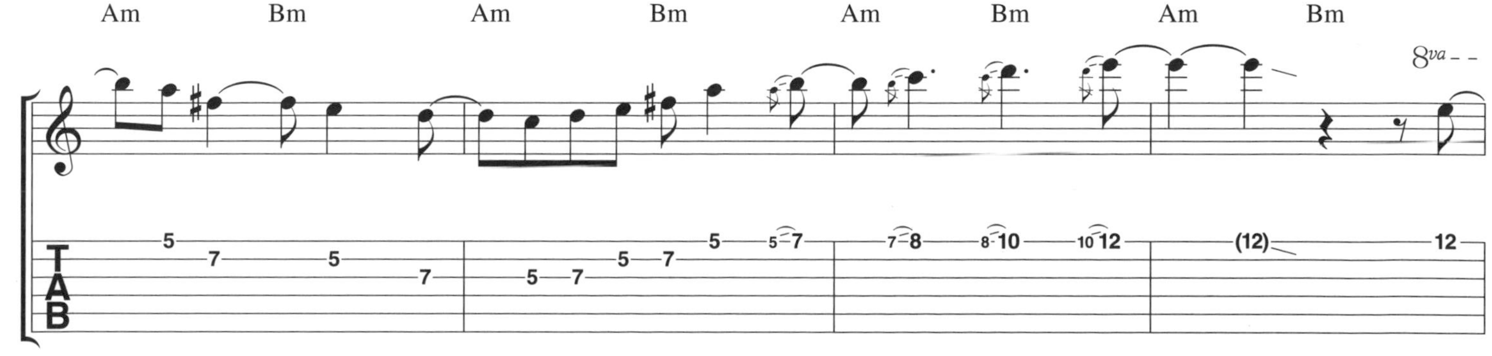
Am Bm Am Bm Am Bm Am Bm
8va

Am Bm Am Bm Am Bm
(8va)
Am Bm Am Bm Am Bm
(8va)
Am Bm Am Bm Am Bm Am Bm
(8va)
Am Bm Am Bm Am Bm
(8va)
Am Bm Am Bm Am Bm Am Bm
(8va)
loco
Pre
let ring
½

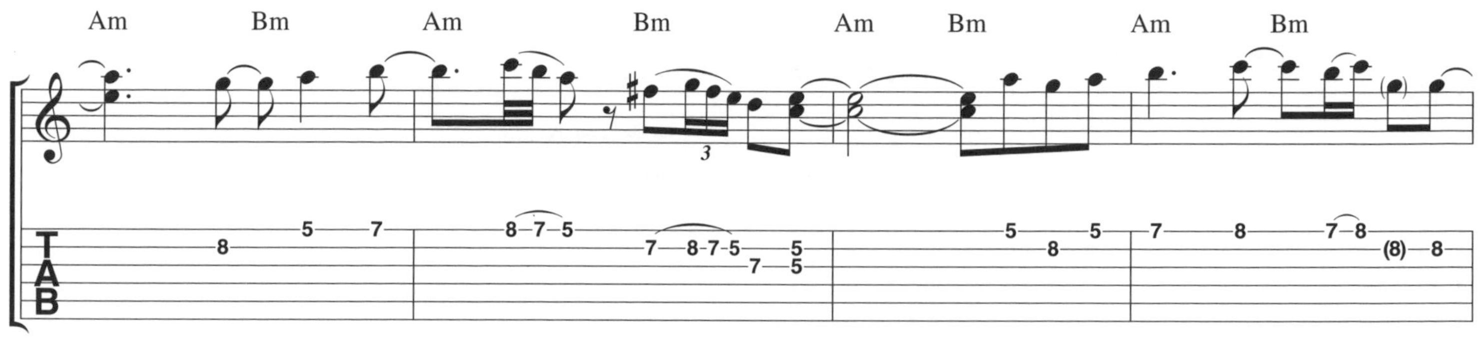
Am Bm Am Bm Am Bm Am Bm
TAB

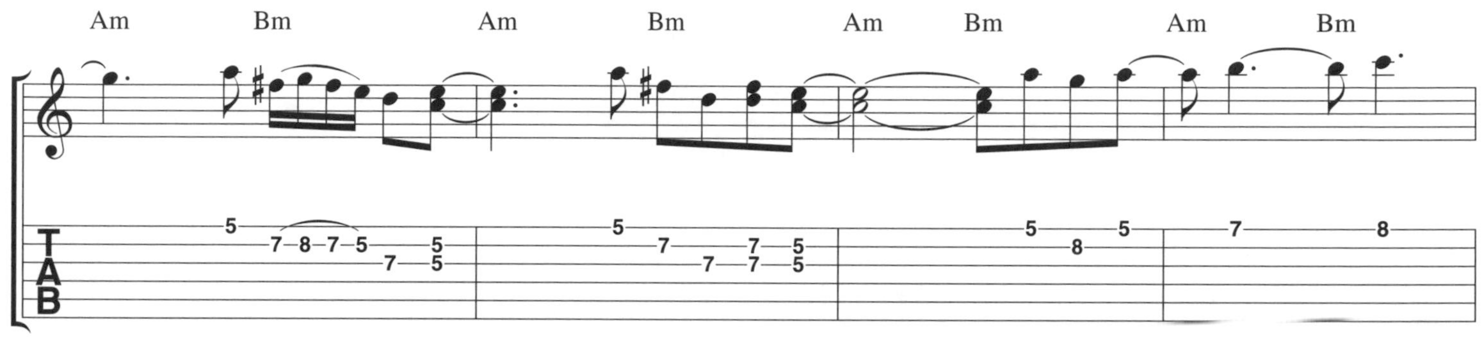
Am Bm Am Bm Am Bm Am Bm
TAB

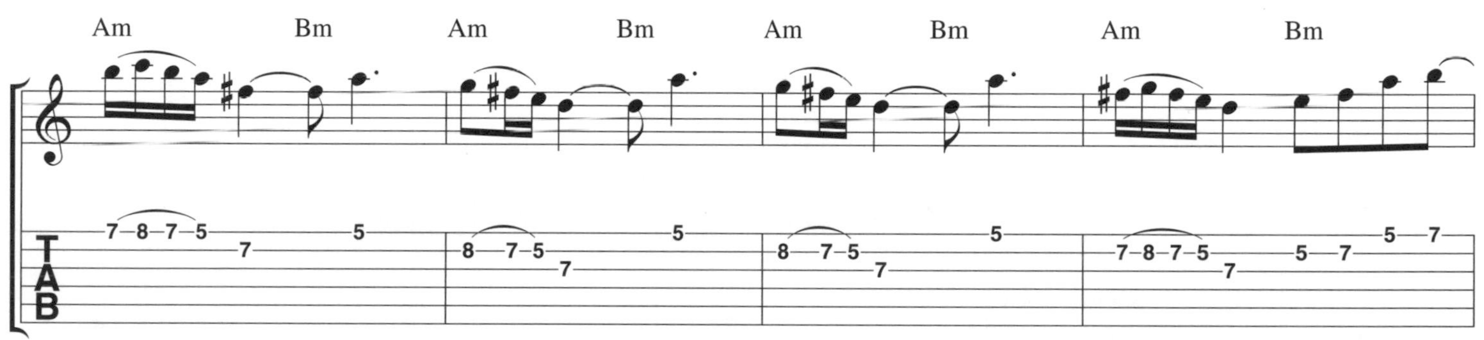
Am Bm Am Bm Am Bm Am Bm
TAB

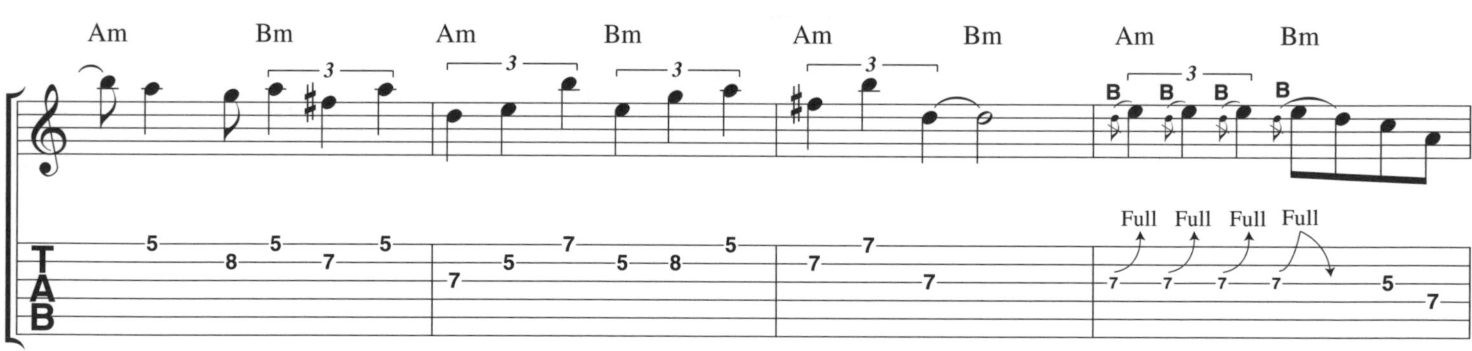
Am Bm Am Bm Am Bm Am Bm
B B B B
Full Full Full Full
TAB

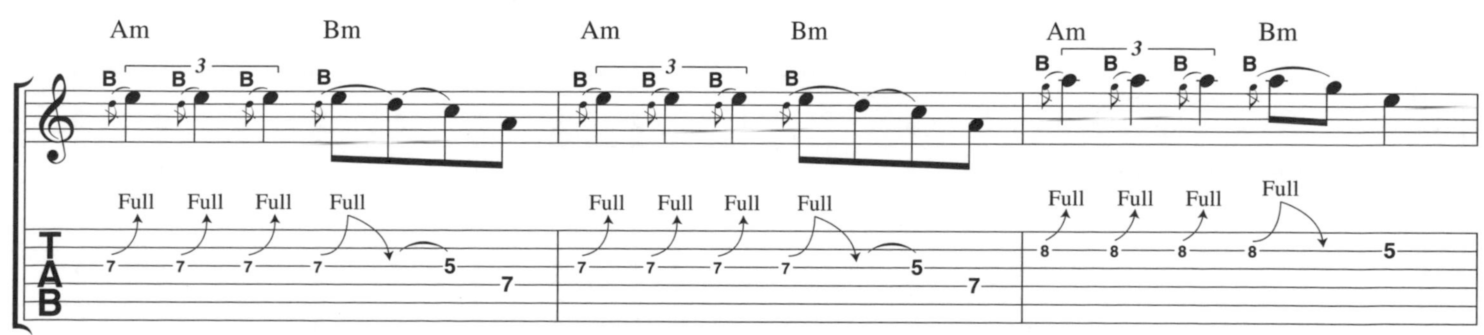
Am Bm Am Bm Am Bm
B B B B B B B B B B B B
Full Full Full Full Full Full Full Full Full Full Full Full
TAB

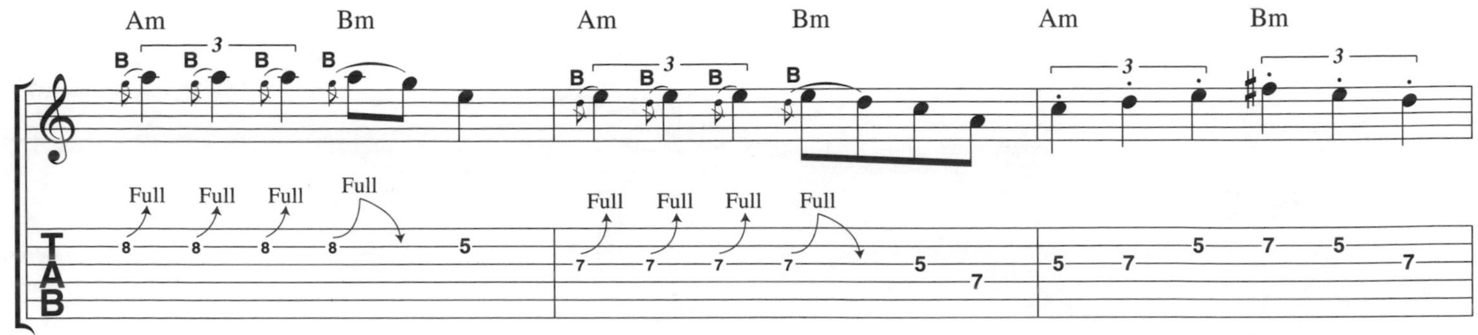

Am
Bm
Am
Bm
Am
Bm
Full

Am
Bm
Am
Bm
Am
Bm

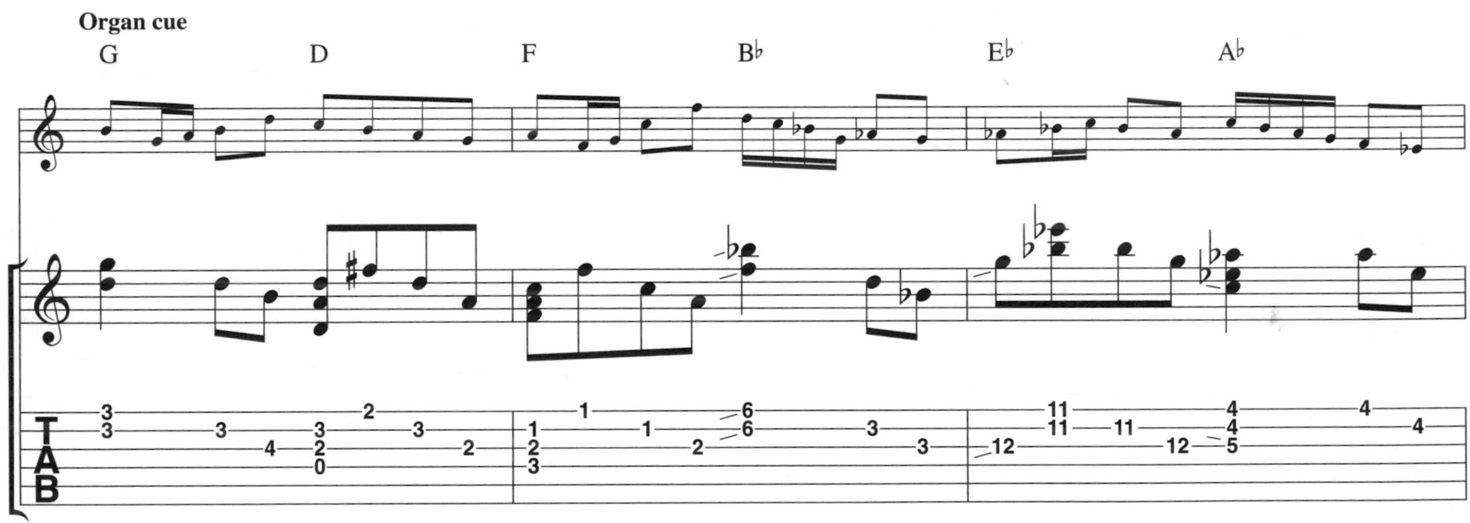

Organ cue
G
D
F
B♭
E♭
A♭

A
3. The

Verse
open
Am
2fr
F♯m
time to hes - i - tate is through,
no time to wal - low in the mire.
know that I would be un - true,
you know that I would be a liar
mf 2° play rhythm slashes

2fr
F♯m
open
Am
Try now we can on - ly lose,
and our
if I was to say to you,

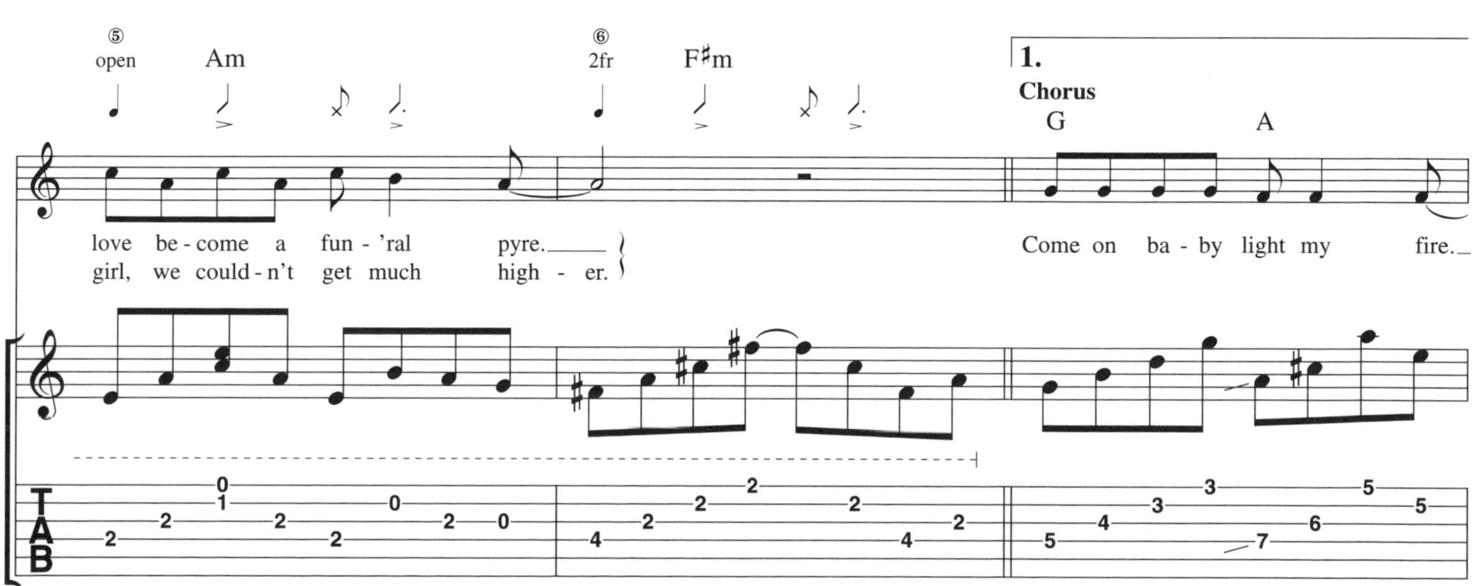
open
Am
2fr
F♯m
1.
Chorus
G
A
love be - come a fun - 'ral pyre.
girl, we could - n't get much high - er.
Come on ba - by light my fire.

1. cont.
D Dsus4 D G A D B
Come on ba - by light my fire.
1. cont.
G D E
Try to set the night on fire. Yeah! 4. You
2. Chorus
G A D Dsus4 D G A
Come on ba - by, light my fire. Come on ba - by, light my fire.
D Dsus4 D F C D Dsus4 D
Try to set the night on fire.

F C D Dsus4 D F C
Try to set the night on fire.
Try to set the night on fire.
D Dsus4 D F C D
Try to set the night on fire.
G D F B♭
E♭ A♭ A

love me two times

Words & Music by The Doors

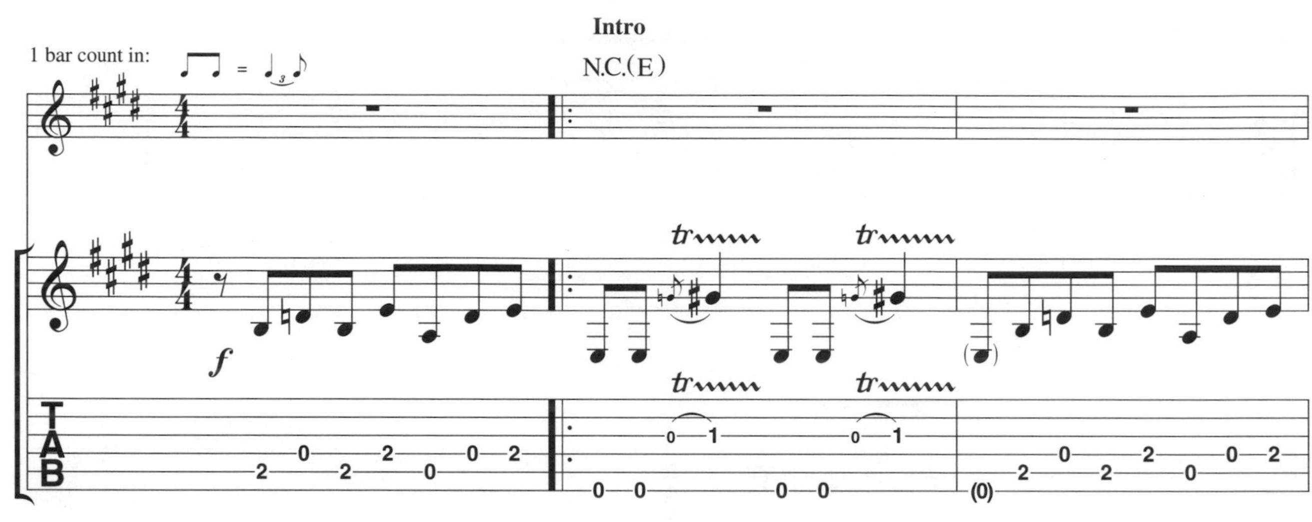

A7
Love me two time girl, I'm goin' a - way.
N.C.(E)
D sus2
Love me two time girl,
one for to - mor - row, one just for to - day.
C7
hold
G
D7sus2
C7
B7
N.C.(E)
Love me two times, I'm goin' a - way.

Verse
2. Love me one time.
Do not speak.
Love me one time.
A7
N.C.(E)
Yeah, my knees got weak.
Love me two times girl,

Dsus2
last me all through the week.
C7 G D7sus2 C7 B7
Love me two times, I'm goin' a - way.
E7♭10 G D7sus2
Love me two times,
C7 B7 N.C.(E)
I'm goin' a - way.
Oh! yeah!
B
½
T
A
B

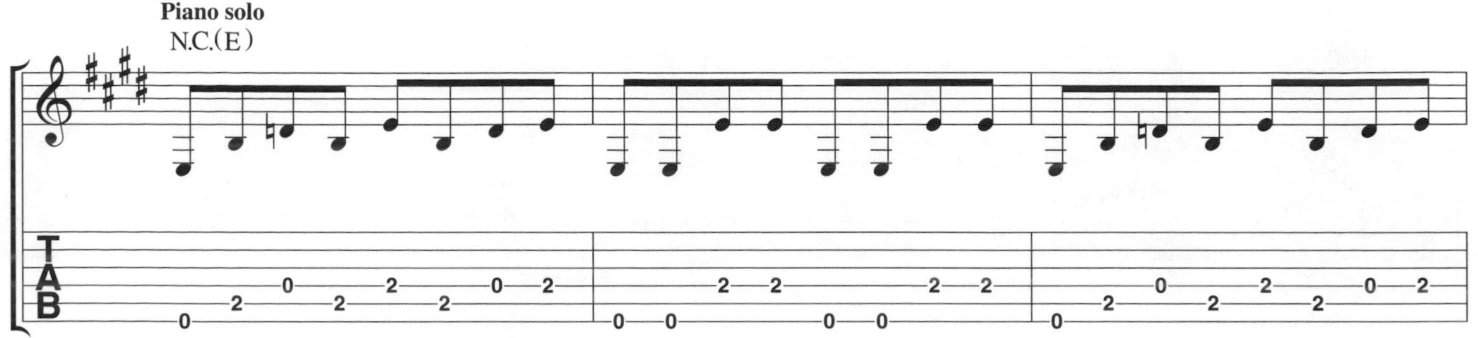
Piano solo
N.C.(E)

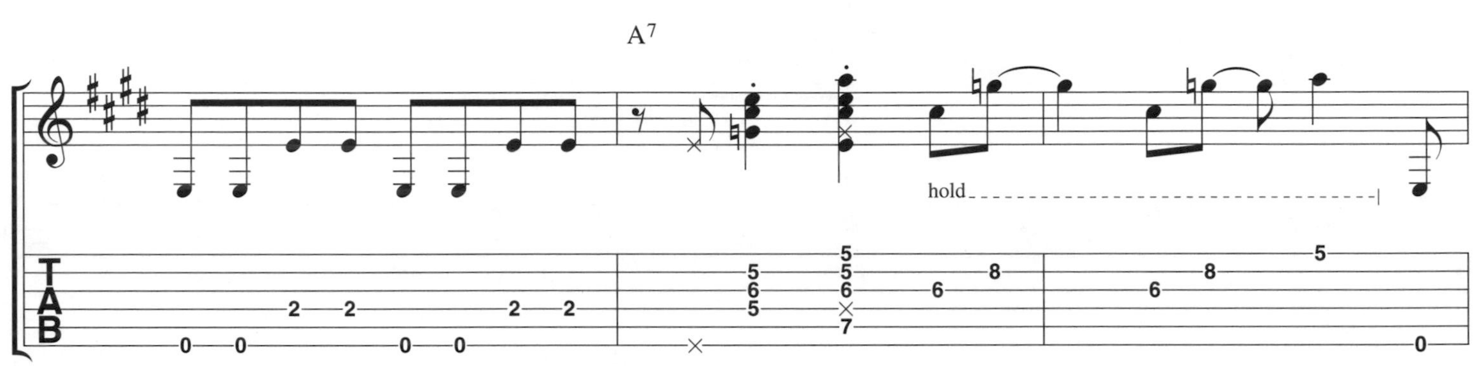
A7
hold

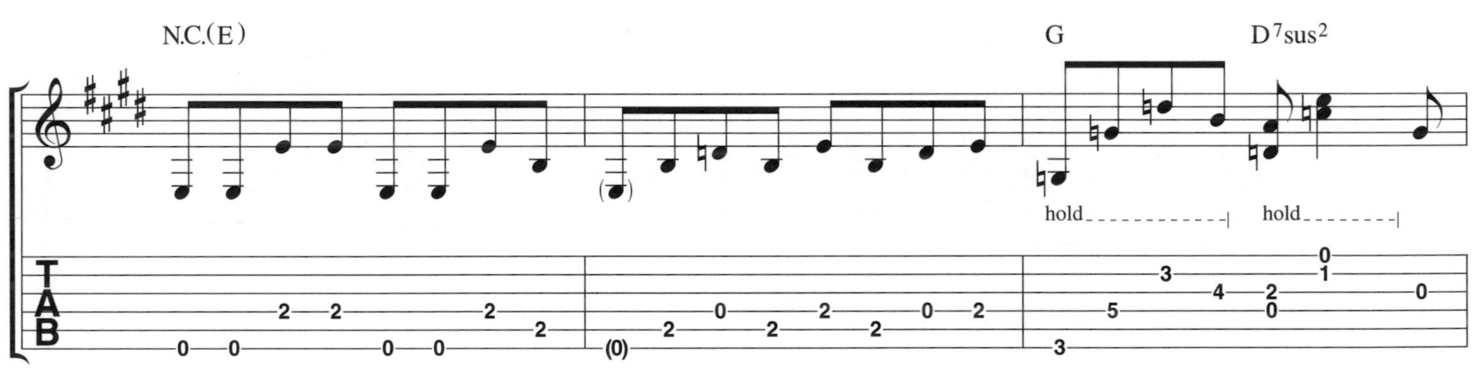
N.C.(E)
G
D7sus2
hold
hold

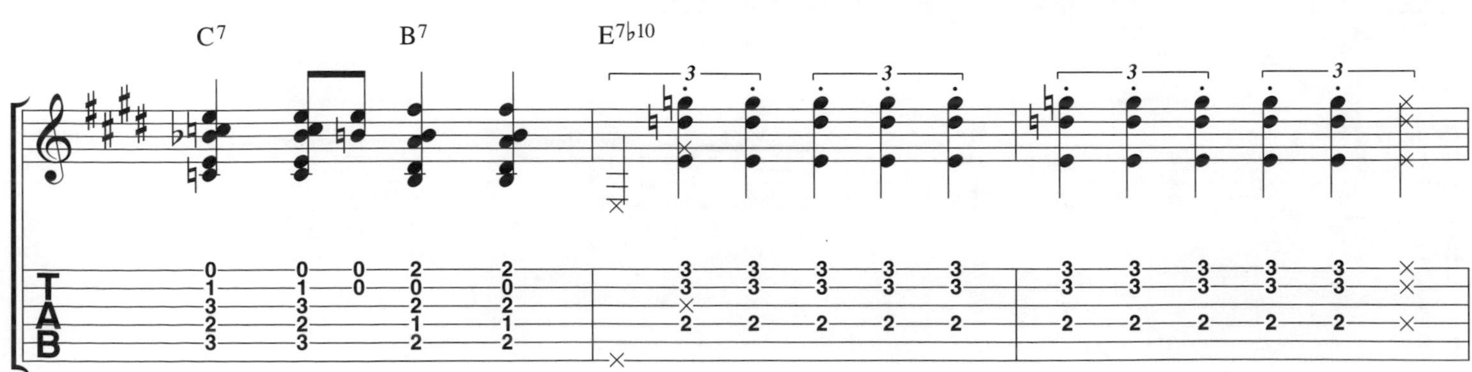
C7
B7
E7♭10

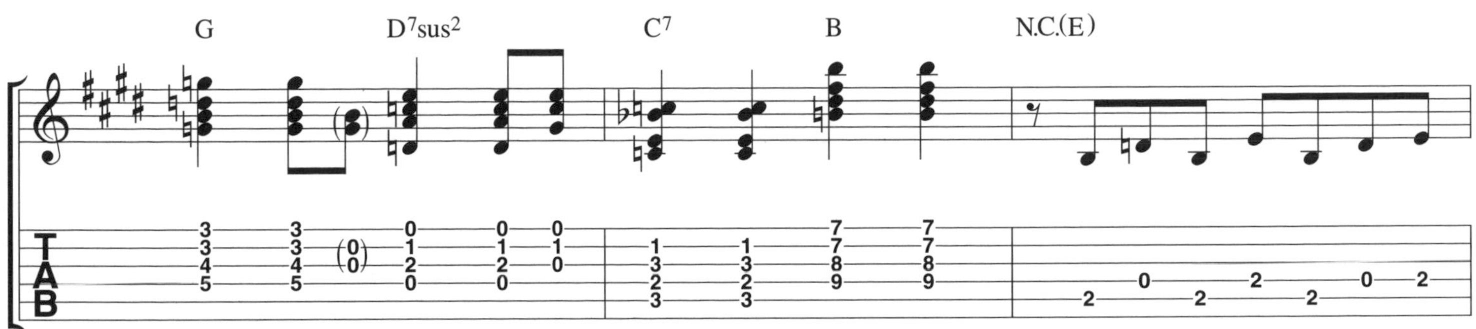
G
D7sus2
C7
B
N.C.(E)

Verse
3. Love me one time.
Could not speak.

A7
Love me one time ba - by.
Pre
½

N.C.(E)
Yeah, my knees got weak.
Love me two time girl.
tr
T
A
B
D7sus2
Last me
B
½
all through the week.
C7
G
D7sus2
Love me two times,
hold bend
C7
B
N.C.(E)
I'm goin' a - way.
Love me two time babe,

love me twice to - day.
hold
A7
Love me two time babe,
'cause I'm goin' a - way.
N.C.(E)
D7sus2
Love me two time girl,
hold
B
½
D7
C7
one for to - mor - row, one just for to - day.
½
hold
3
3

G D7 D7sus2 C7 B E7♭10
Love me two times, I'm goin' a - way.
G D7sus2 C7 B
Love me two times, I'm goin' a - way.
E7♭10 G D7sus2
Love me two times, I'm
C7 B7 E7♭10
goin' a - way.
8va
T
A
B

roadhouse blues

Words by Jim Morrison
Music by The Doors

up - on the wheel. Keep your
eyes on the road, your hands up - on the wheel.
Yeah, we're goin' to the road - house, gon - na have a real old
a good time.
B
¼

Yeah, in
back of the road - house they got some_ bun - ga - lows.__
Yeah, in back of the road - house they got some_ bun - ga - lows._
And that's for the peo - ple who

like to go down slow.
Let it a-
Chorus
(A7)
roll, ba-by roll.
Let it a-roll, ba-by roll.
Let it a-roll, ba-by roll.
Let it a-
B
roll,
C
B
all-night
Solo
N.C.(E)
long.
ff
Full
B

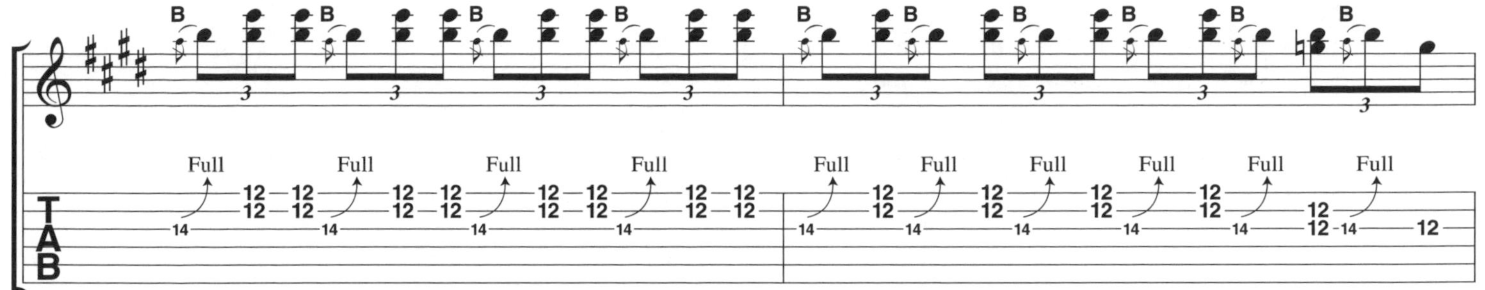
B
Full
12
14
T
A
B
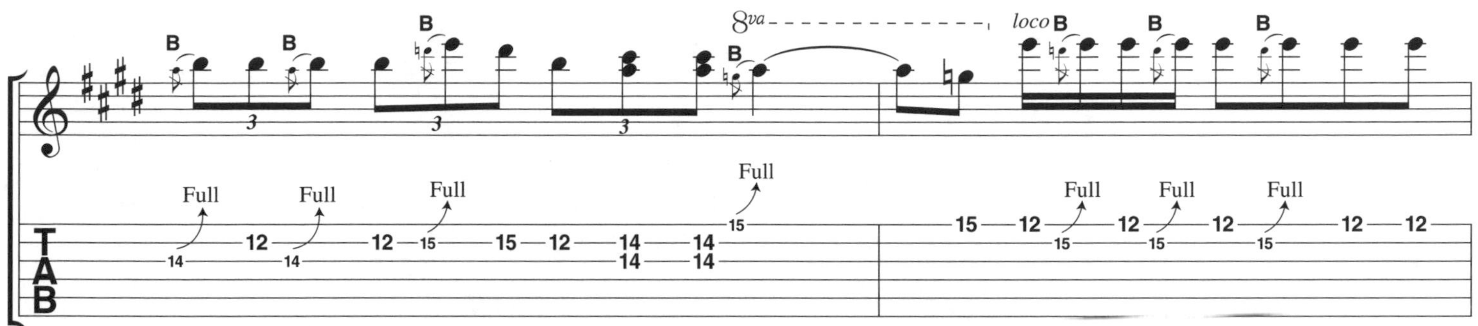
8va
loco
B
Full
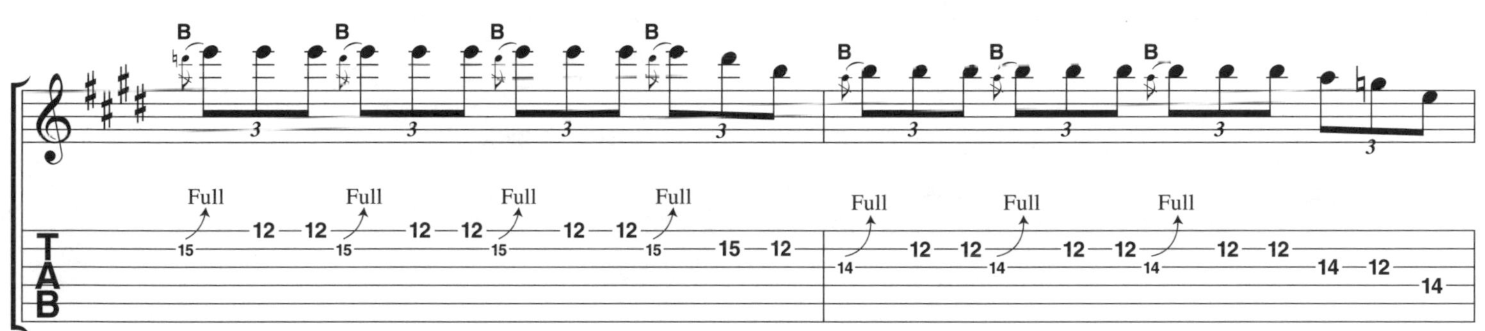
B
Full
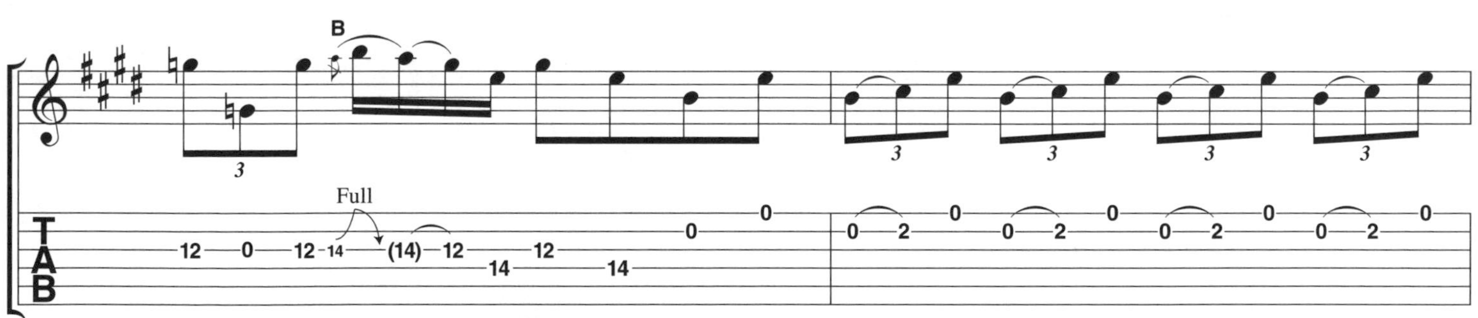
B
Full
(14)
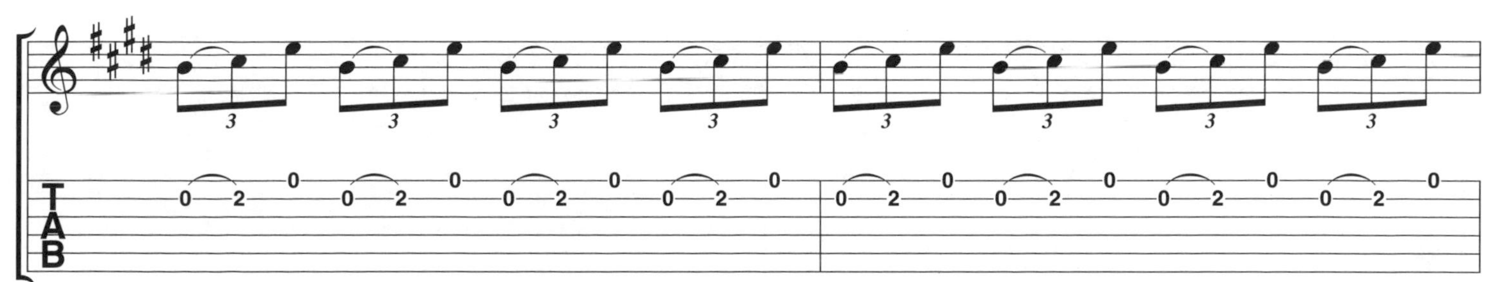

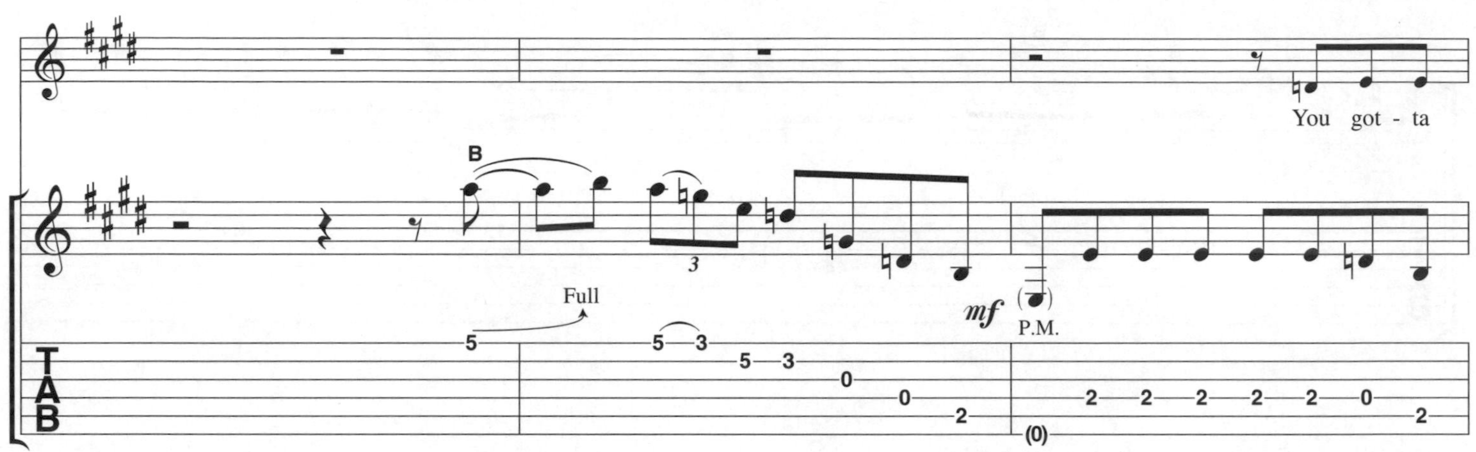
You got - ta
B
Full
mf
P.M.

roll, roll, roll, you got - ta thrill__ my soul al - right.
Ashen lady Ashen lady
P.M.
sim.

Roll, roll, roll, roll a - through my soul__ I got - ta
give up your vows. Give

peep - a - con - ya chou chum,
up your vows.
paw cork cork, I got - ta
hay - cha - coon - a - may - cha,
Save our city,
ba - ba loo la hay ahow,
bow pa key chow
save our city
ee sown comp, yeah
right
right.
now.
1.
1. cont.
2.
E7
f
2. Well I

woke up this morn - ing, I got my - self a beer.
Yeah, I woke up this morn - ing and I got my - self a beer.
The fu-ture's un - cer-tain and the
end is al - ways near.
Let it

Chorus
N.C.(A7)
roll, ba - by roll. Let it a - roll, ba - by roll.
Let it a - roll, ba - by roll. Let it a -
B
B C C♯ D D♯
roll, hey, all night
E (N.C.)
E9
long.
8va
Full
Full

riders on the storm

Words & Music by The Doors

D
C
Em
dog with-out a bone an act - or out on loan. Ri - ders on the storm. 2. There's a
cancel trem.
Verse
Em
kil - ler on the road his brain is squirm-ing like a toad.
Am
Take a long hol - i - day,
Em
D
let your child - ren play. If you give this man a ride, sweet

C
Em
fam - i - ly will die.
Kil - ler on the road,
yeah.
Solo
Em
w/tremolo fx
Am
Em
D
C
Em
mp
cancel trem.
3. Girl, you

Verse
got - ta have your man.
Girl you got - ta have your man.
Am
Take him by the hand,
Em
make him un - der - stand.
D
The world on you de - pends our
C
life will nev - er end.
Em
Got - ta love your man.
Yeah.

Piano solo

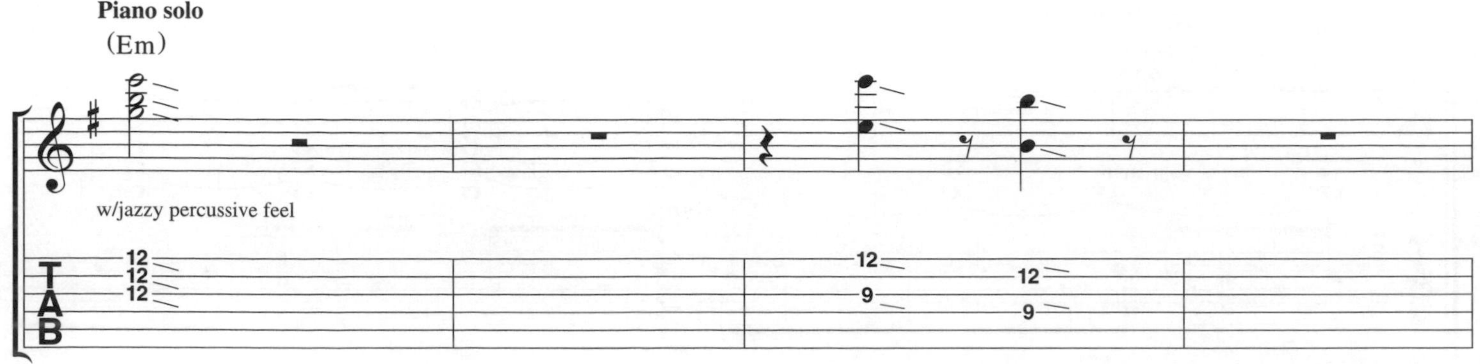

(Em)
w/jazzy percussive feel

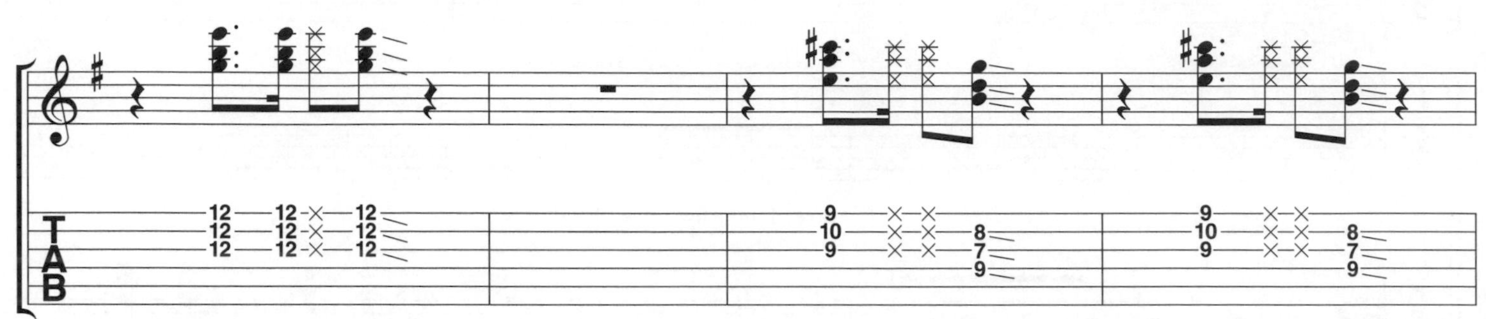

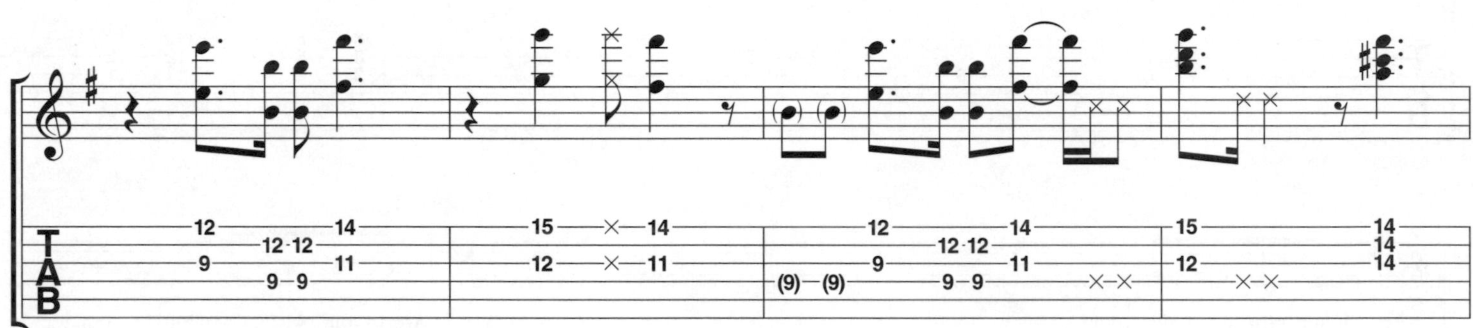

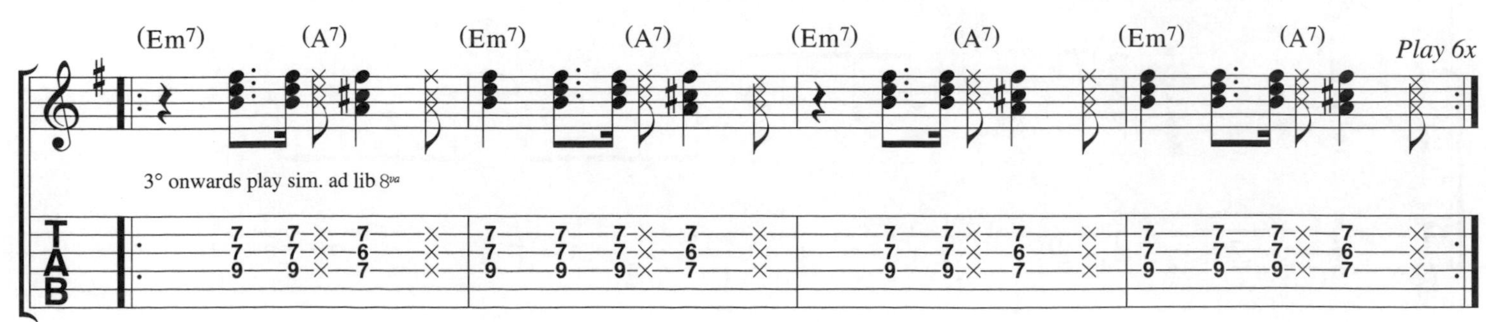

(Em7)
(A7)
(Em7)
(A7)
(Em7)
(A7)
(Em7)
(A7)
Play 6x
3° onwards play sim. ad lib 8va

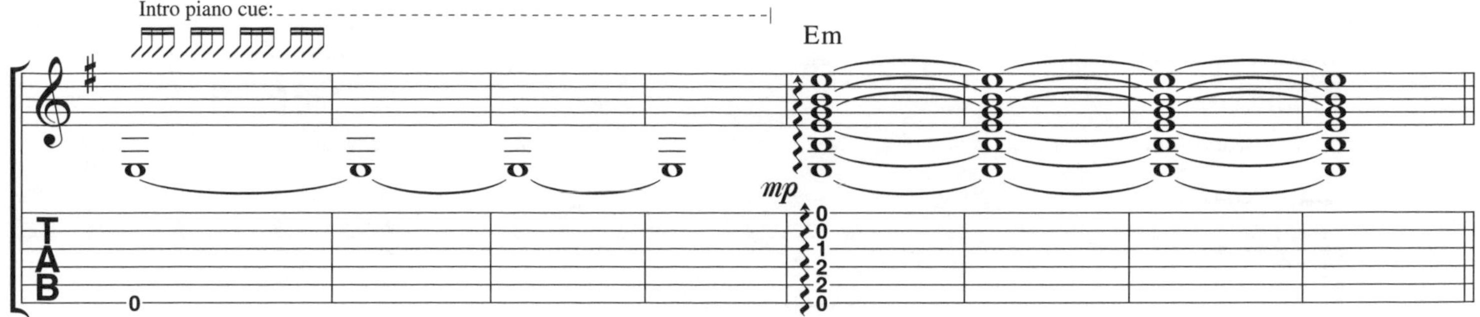
Intro piano cue:
Em
mp

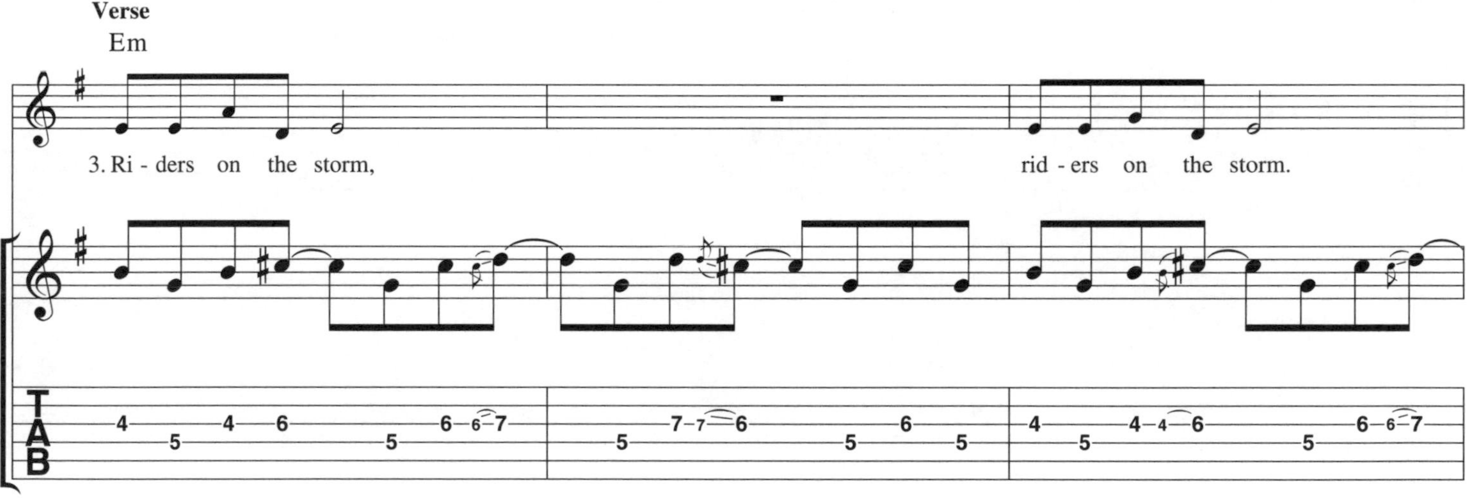
Verse
Em
3. Ri - ders on the storm,
rid - ers on the storm.

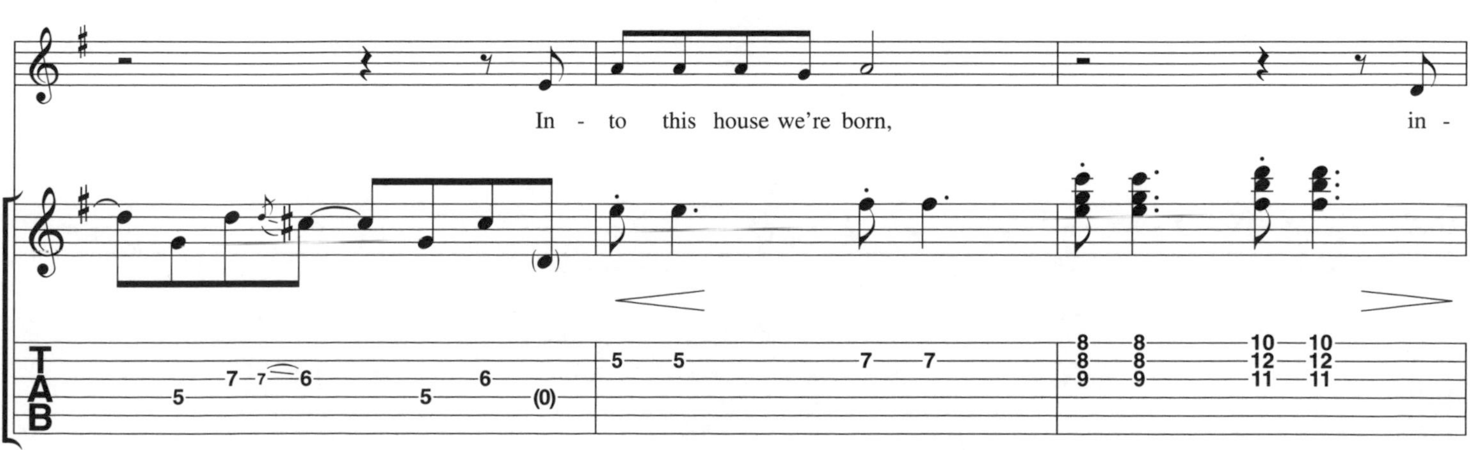
In - to this house we're born,
in -

Em
D
- to this world we're thrown.
Like a dog with - out a bone an

C
Em
act - or out on loan.
Rid - ers on the storm.

Outro solo

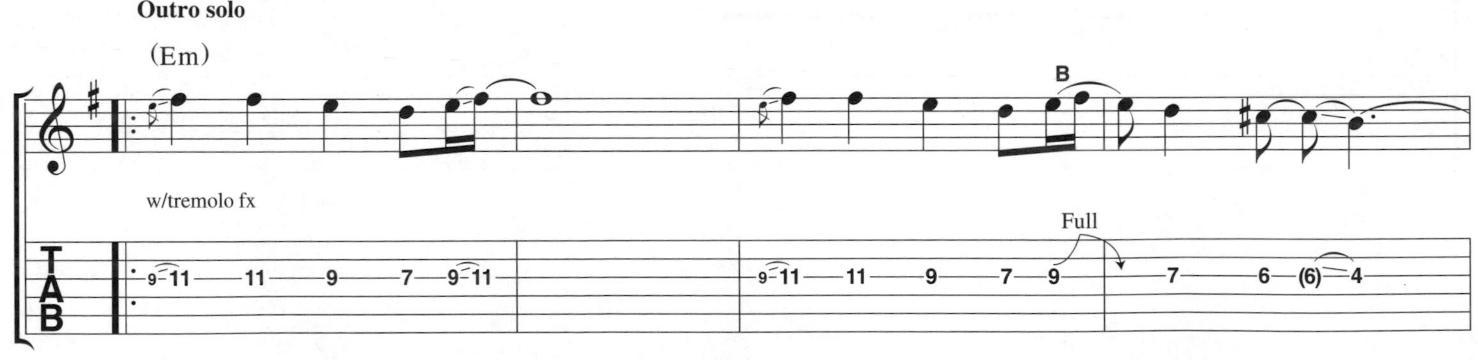
(Em)
w/tremolo fx
Full

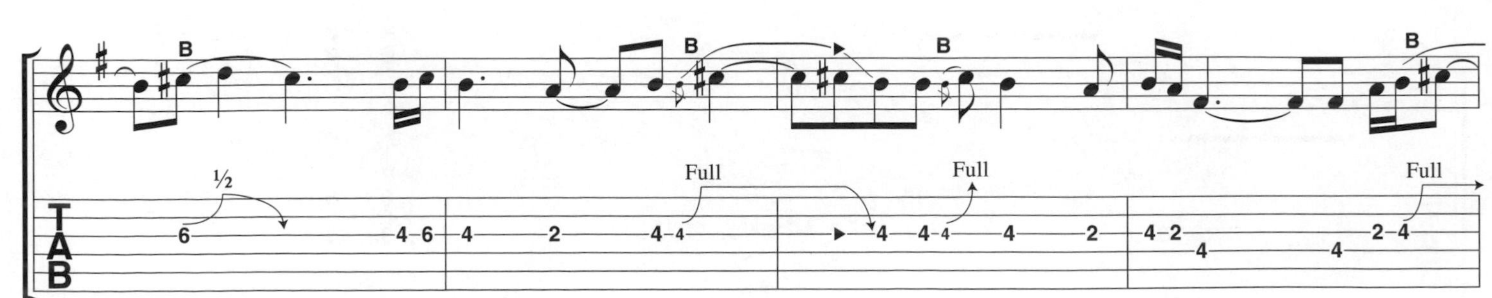
½
Full
Full
Full

Rid - ers on the storm.
Rid - ers on the storm.
B
B
Full
Full
Full
11 11 9 7 9
7
2 4

Rid - ers on the storm.
B
B
Full
1½
6 7 6 4 2
4 2 4 2 4 2
4 2 4
2 4 2 4 4

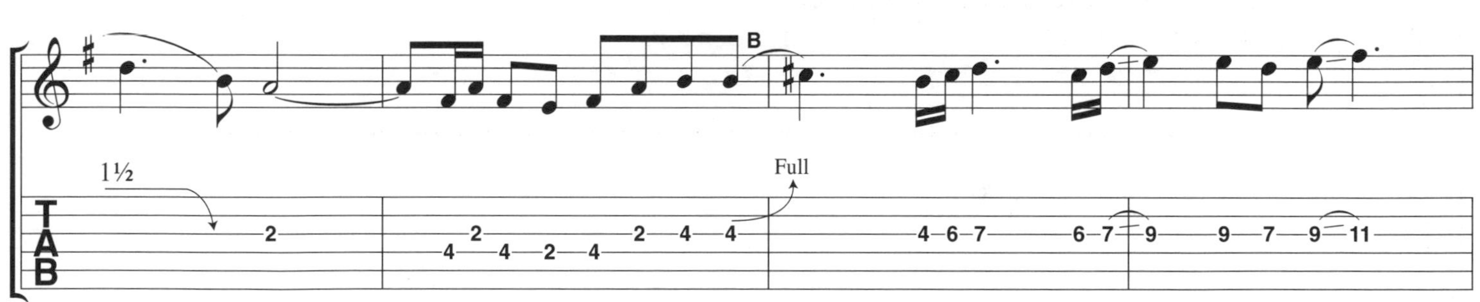
B
1½
Full
2
2 4 4 2 4 2 4 4
4 6 7 6 7 9 9 7 9 11

B
B
Repeat ad lib to fade
½
½
9 11
9 11
12 12 12
14 14 14

spanish caravan

Words & Music by The Doors

Intro
Freely

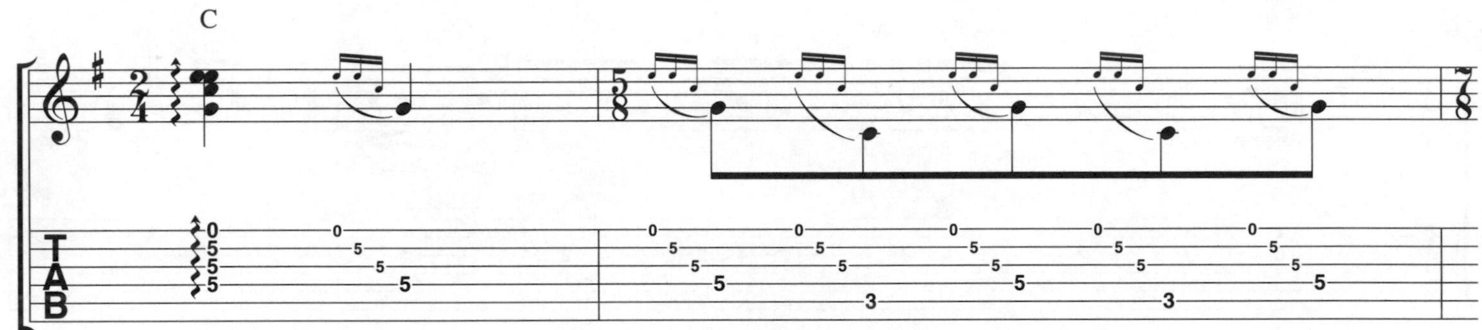

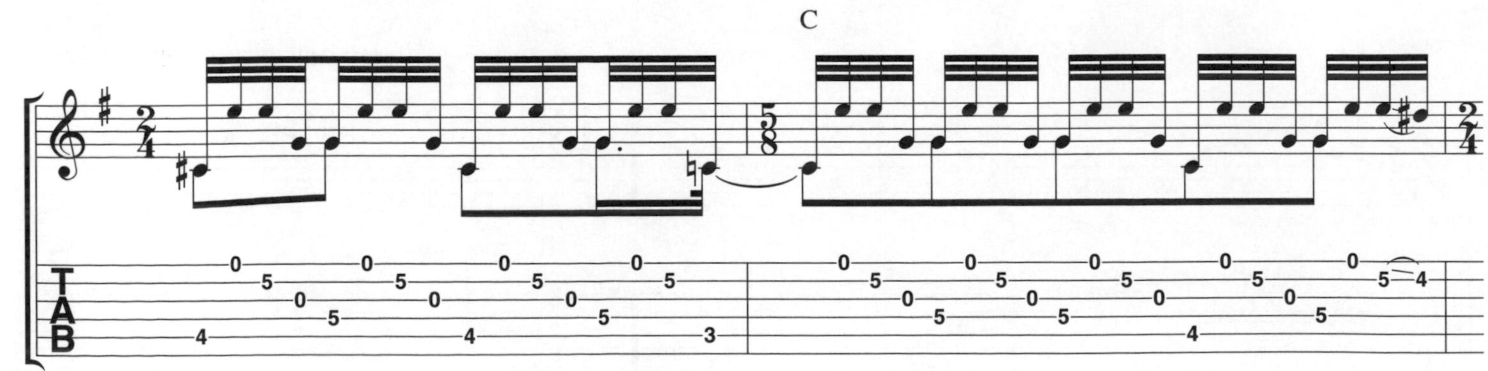

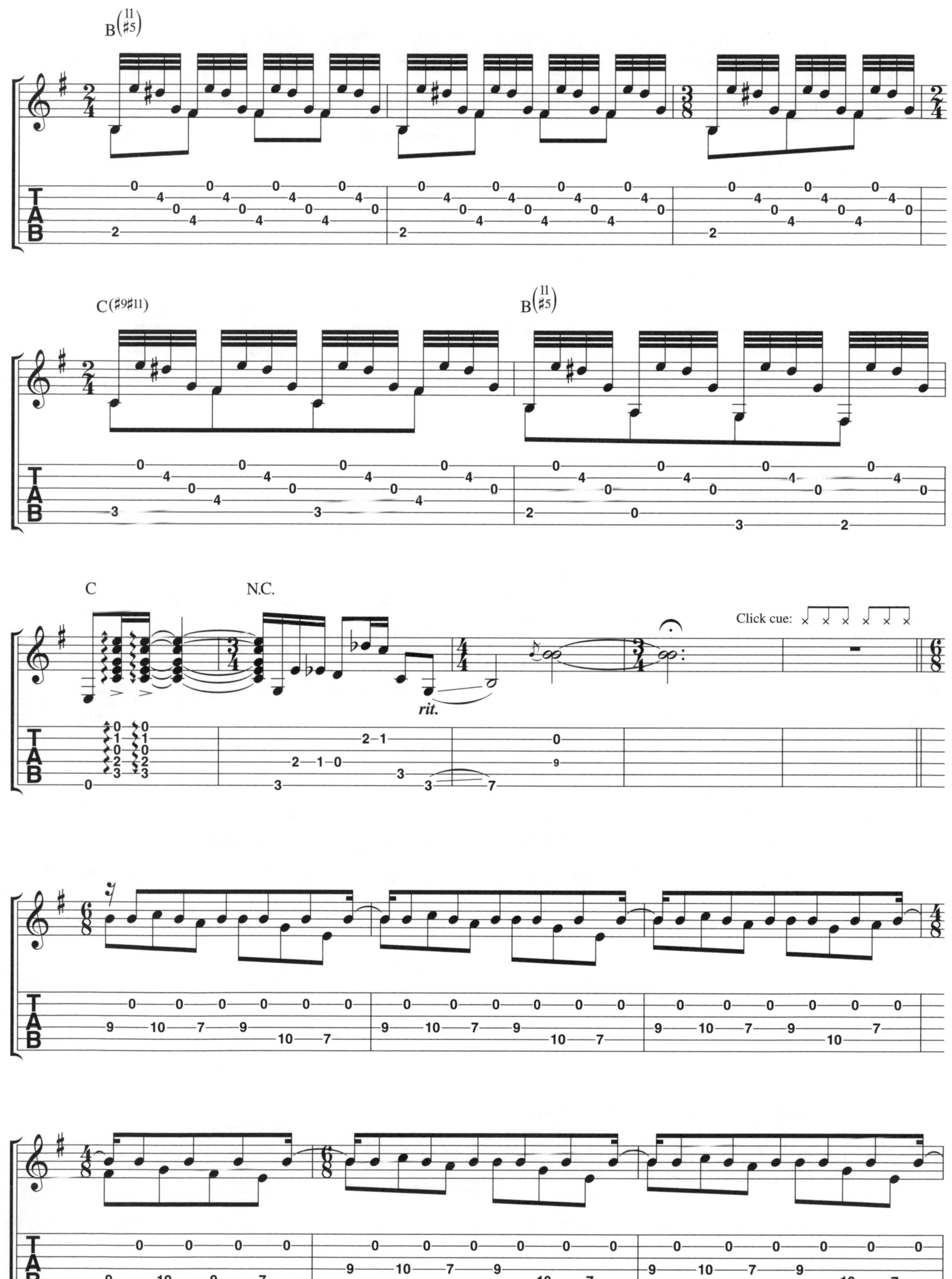

B(11 ♯5)
C(♯9♯11)
B(11 ♯5)
C
N.C.
rit.
Click cue:

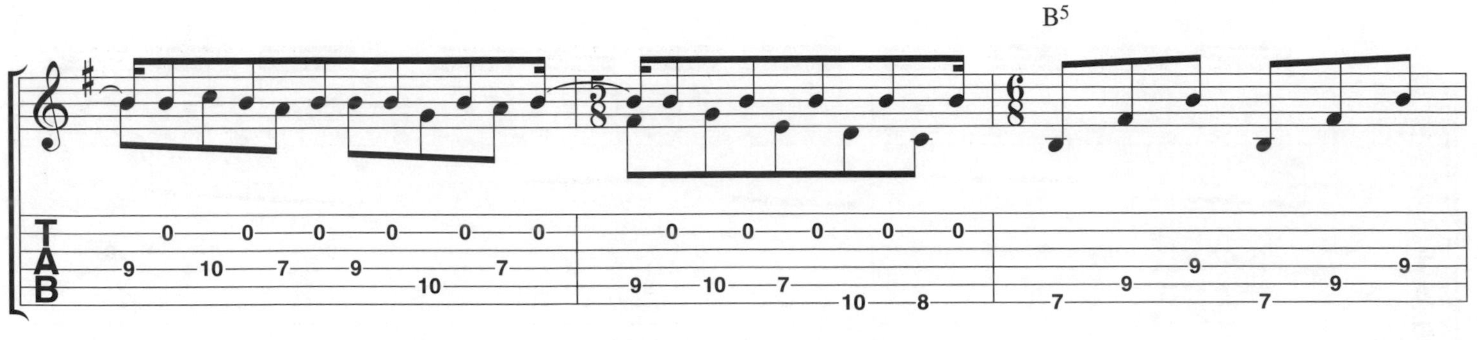
B5
T
A
B

C7
B5
T
A
B

Am7
D
T
A
B

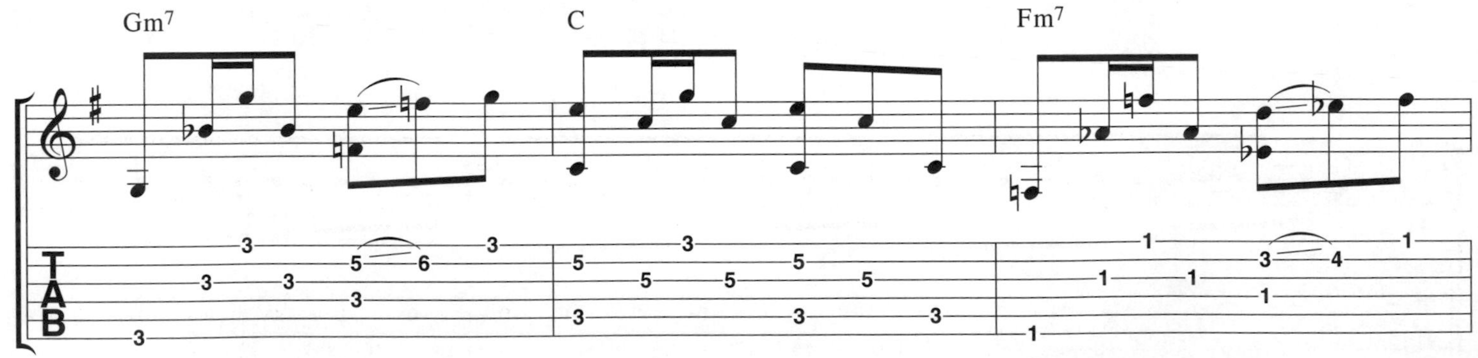
Gm7
C
Fm7
T
A
B

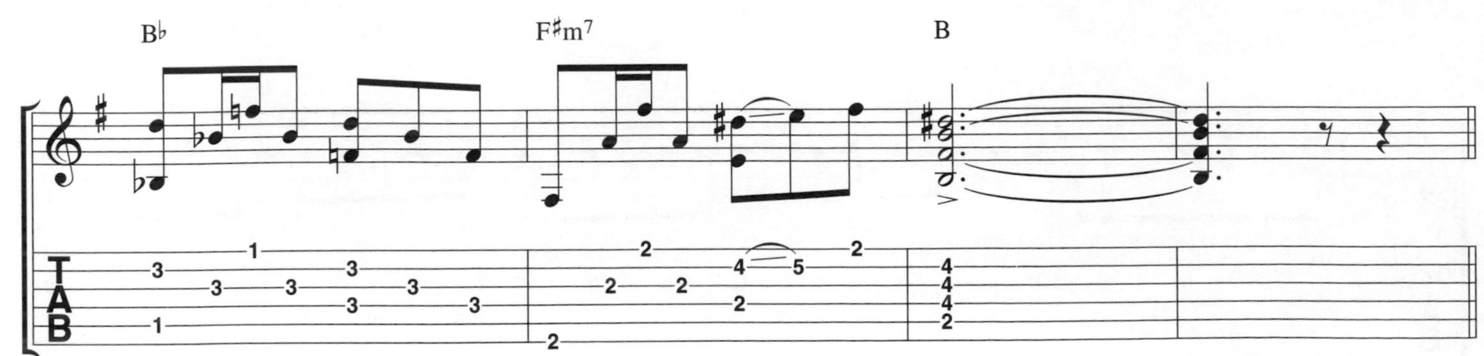
B♭
F♯m7
B
T
A
B

Verse
Em Am B7 Em
Car - ry me car - a - van, take me a - way.
Em Am B7 Em
Take me to Por - tu - gal, take me to Spain.
Am Em B7/F♯ Em
An - da - lu - si - a with fields full of grain.
Am Em/B B7/F♯ Em
I have to see you a - gain and a - gain.

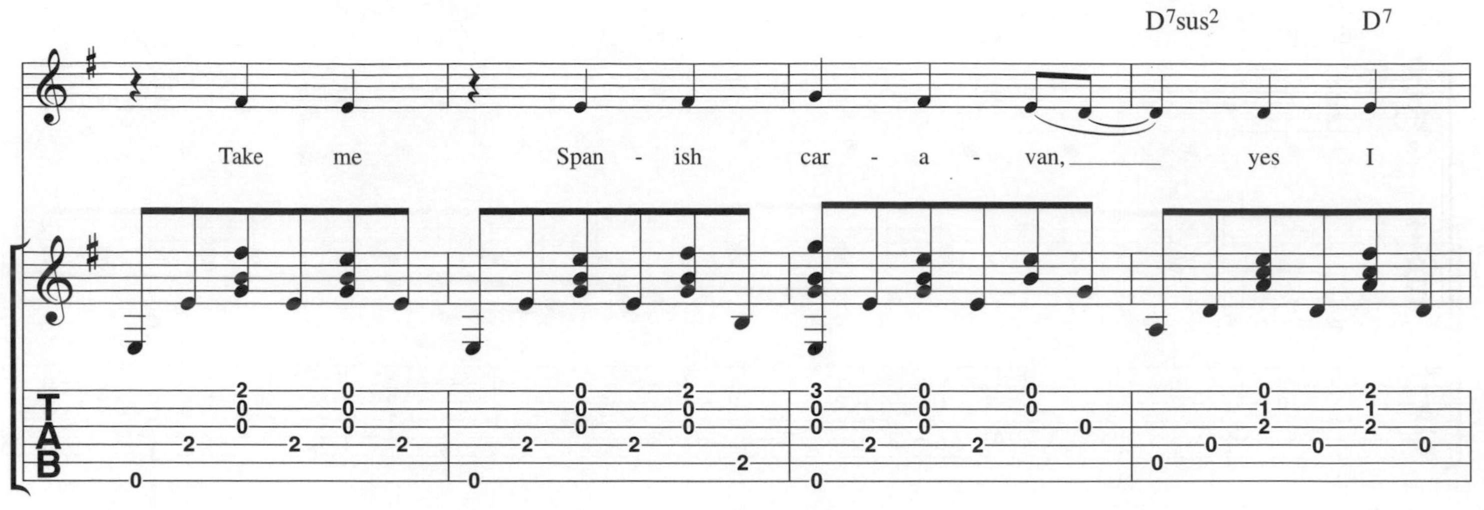
D7sus2
D7
Take me Span - ish car - a - van, yes I

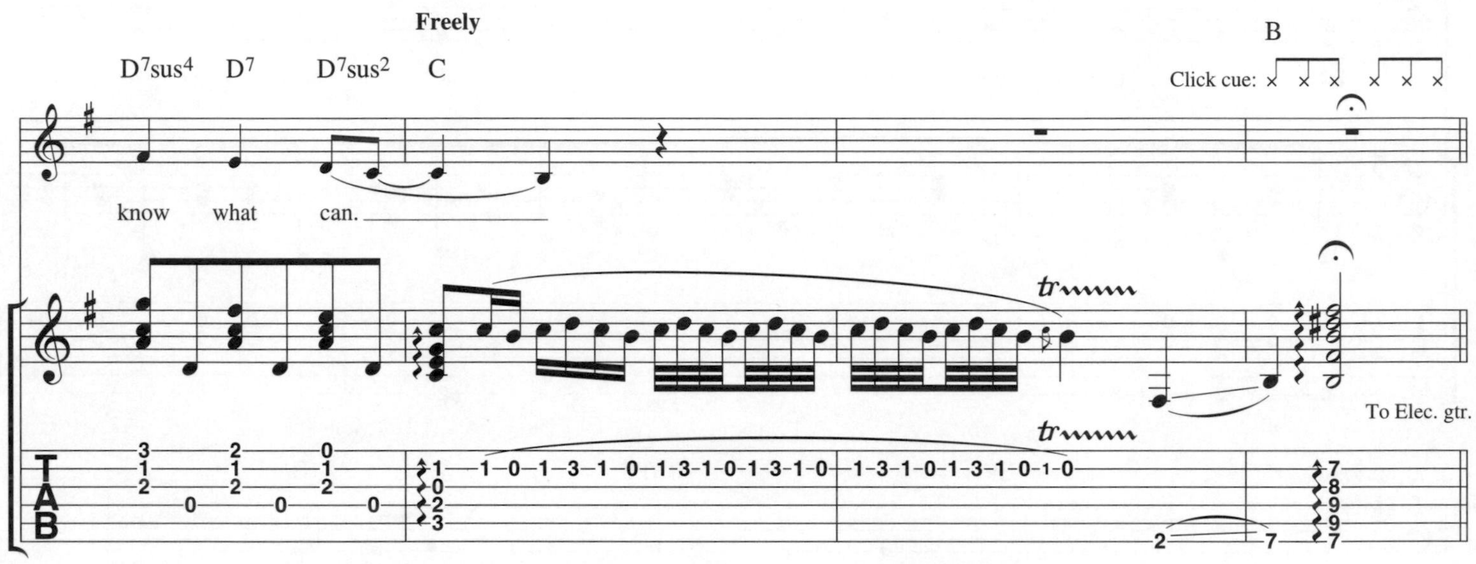
Freely
D7sus4
D7
D7sus2
C
B
Click cue:
know what can.
To Elec. gtr.

a tempo
w/distortion & fuzz

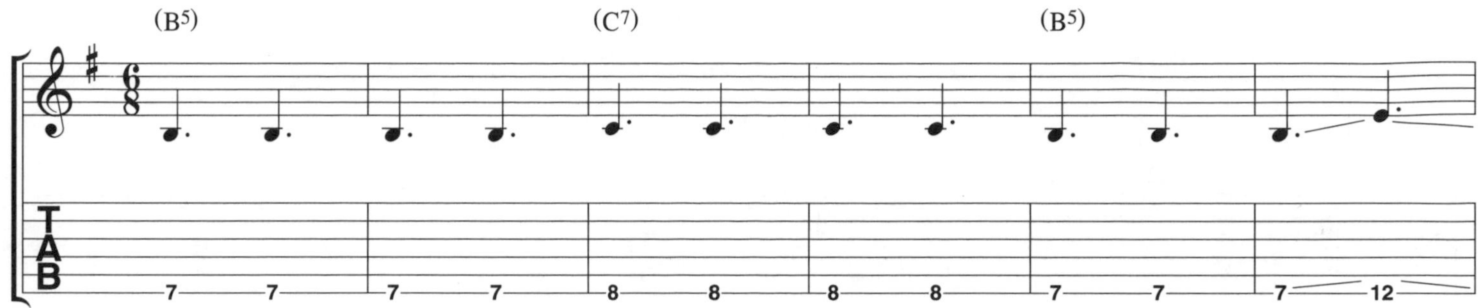
(B5)
(C7)
(B5)

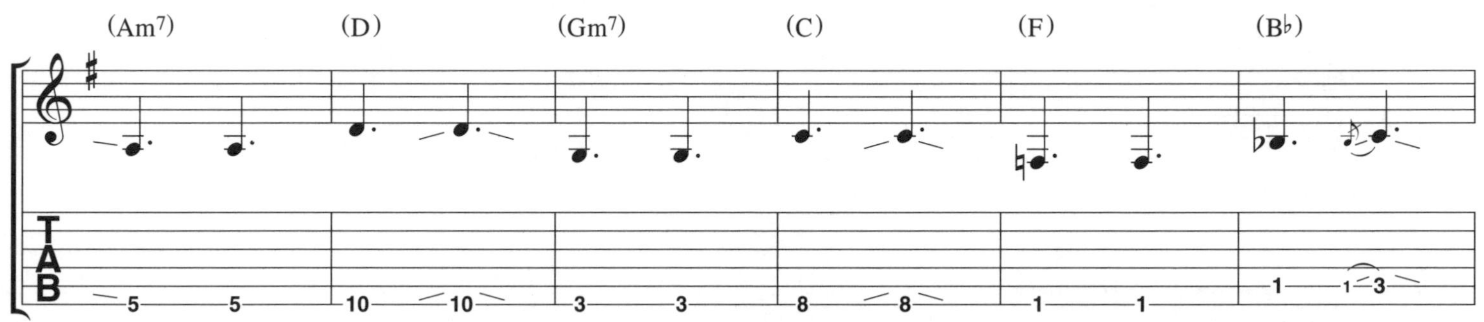
(Am7)
(D)
(Gm7)
(C)
(F)
(B♭)

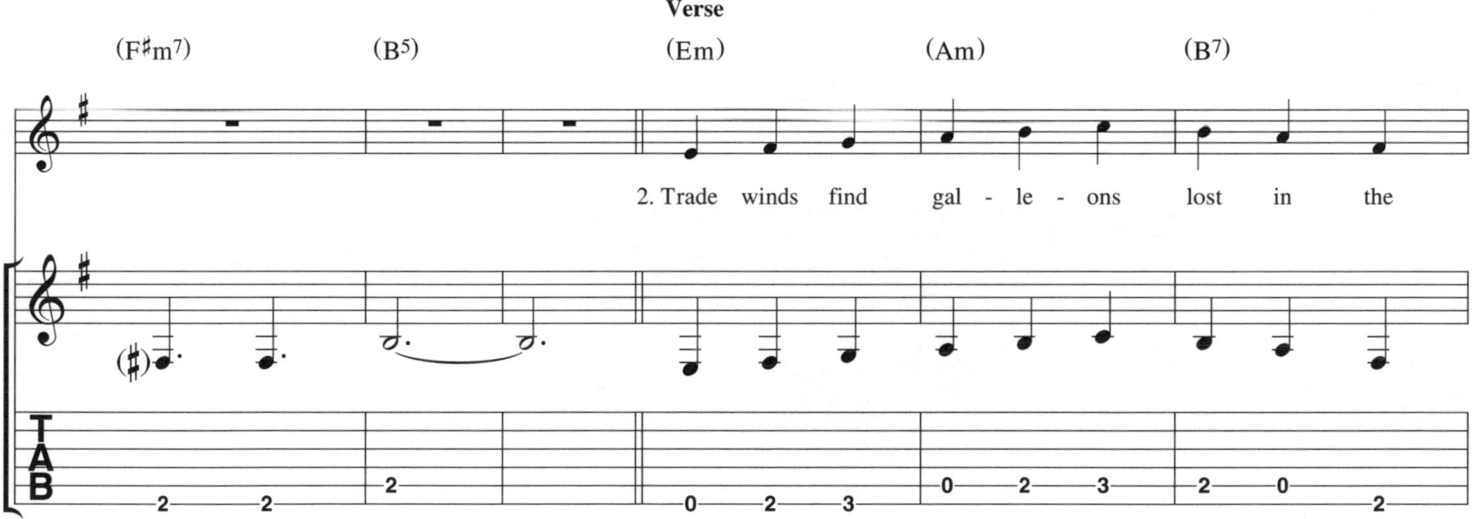
Verse
(F♯m7)
(B5)
(Em)
(Am)
(B7)
2. Trade winds find gal - le - ons lost in the

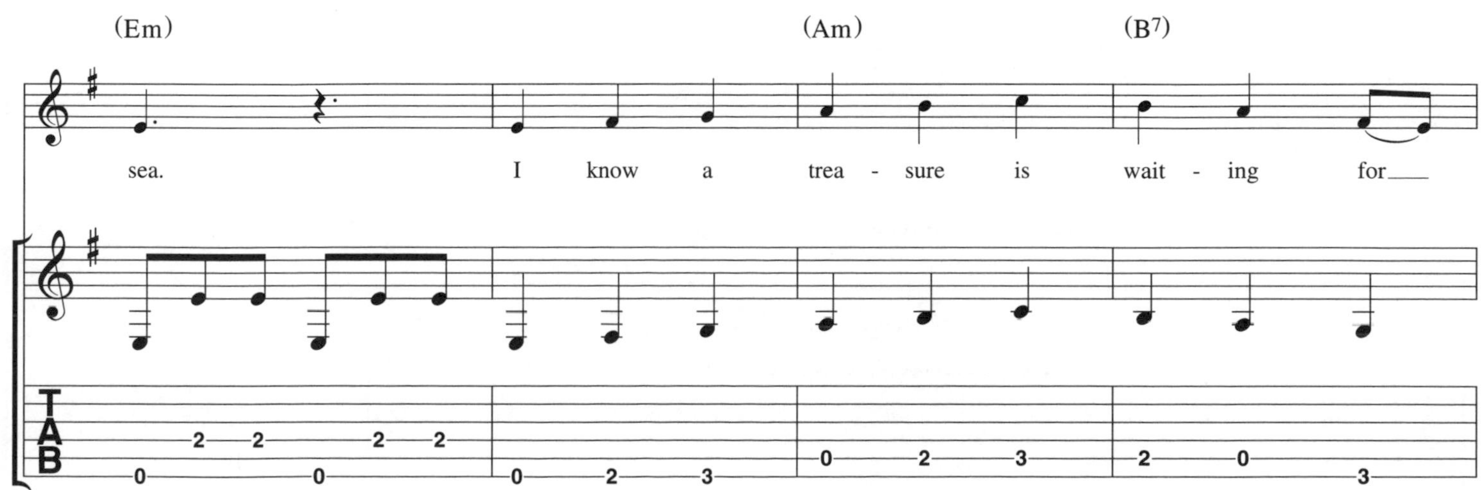
(Em)
(Am)
(B7)
sea. I know a trea - sure is wait - ing for

(Em)
(Am)
(Em)
(B7/F♯)
me. Sil - ver and gold and the moun - tains of
(Em)
(Am)
(Em/B)
(B7add11/F♯)
Spain. I have to see you a - gain and a -
(Em)
(D7)
- gain. Take me Span - ish car - a - van, yes I
(C)
(Em)
know you can.